Calling from the Heart

———————o

AN INVITATION
TO YOUR
SOUL COMPANION

———————o

A SHAMANIC CALLING CEREMONY
BASED ON THE TEACHINGS OF
WILL ROCKINGBEAR

———————o

Cathy,
Blessings on your
Journey!
Love,
White Star

Calling from the Heart

AN INVITATION
TO YOUR
SOUL COMPANION

A Shamanic Calling Ceremony
Based on the Teachings of
Will Rockingbear

Robin White Star

INWORD
PUBLISHERS

For more information please contact:
Robin White Star
www.FlowerEagle.com

Cover Artwork: Sharon Hardin
Author Photo: Cienna Grady
Cover and Interior Design: Bhakti-rasa

Inword Publishers
inwordpublishers.com
info@inwordpublishers.com

Contents

Introduction

INVITATION TO YOUR SOUL COMPANION

MY JOURNEY

Echoing the steady beating of my heart, the sound of the Tarahumara Drum sent deep reverberations through me. The drum's even, rhythmical pulse relaxed and focused my breathing while creating wave after wave of energy that coursed along my spine, into my soft, inner parts, my lungs, my heart and my brain. I breathed in its deep percussive voice and became one with its pulsating waves of energy. I was reminded that throughout time humans have experienced a special relationship with the drum, in ceremony and in communicating with the spirits and in communicating with each other. The beat of the drum mirrors the heartbeat of Mother Earth and, like a young child, we are sustained and nurtured by the beating heart of our Mother. I was deep in the Calling Ceremony for which I had been consciously preparing for many months, and in some ways years. The beat of the drum was comforting me, filling me with strength and purpose and, like a canoe, transporting me into the Invisible World where I would meet my Soul Companion, my Beloved, whom I was calling into my life.

That cold but clear day in January 2000 found me sitting cross-legged in front of a wood stove, gazing steadily into a strong, radiant fire in the Earth Green Medicine Lodge in the Black Mountains of Western North Carolina. My teacher, Will Rockingbear of Cherokee descent and a spiritual teacher and healer, was conducting the Calling Ceremony at my request. Rockingbear had come to the Black Mountains in the 1980s and had created a community of students and apprentices (apprentices are students who request to go deeper with the teachings in order to become teachers and healers themselves). Through native teachings, traditions, and ceremonies, Rockingbear was showing us how to more fully live our lives as Sacred Human Beings, healing ourselves and others, in a never-ending spiral of conscious spiritual growth. He called this the Beauty Way. I had been studying with Rockingbear for more than 4 years at this point, sitting in circle with him and other healers on Monday nights. So, for me, requesting the Calling Ceremony was the next step on my journey of inner healing and self-realization.

I had come to the Blue Ridge Mountains of Western North Carolina a few years earlier after repeatedly seeing blue, hazy mountains in visions while drumming for the personal growth classes I was teaching at The Jung Center in Houston, Texas. The mountains were beckoning me, telling me to "Come, come be with us. We want you to come live with us." I wasn't sure which mountains they were or where they were located. At that time, I didn't know that I could have asked them directly! I was simply receiving the message, not actually in dialogue with the Mountain Beings. Several months later while watching the movie *Last of the Mohicans* with my sister, I immediately recognized the mountains as those in my visions and simply had to wait until the end of the movie to see where it was filmed – the Blue Ridge Mountains of

North Carolina. When my parents got wind of my desire to move, they decided to join me and my young son and, together, the four of us moved to the Asheville area of Western North Carolina.

It was never my conscious intention to travel down the path of Native Traditions; I was led to it through the appearance of Dragonfly in my life. And, of course, before then, many other teachers and teachings paved the way for this new path. First, I began my spiritual training with the Inner Peace Movement when I was 13 years old in Dayton, Ohio. Along with my family, I experienced inner discovery courses and spiritual leadership training that prepared me to lecture and tour throughout the United States, Canada and Puerto Rico and to eventually teach those same courses at the various IPM conference centers. When I left my work with the Inner Peace Movement after 16 years, I settled in Houston, Texas, to be close to my family. My path was no longer feeding me in the way I needed and I returned to my family in order to regroup and set a new direction. After many months of self-reflection, I asked Great Spirit for a new spiritual direction – a path that was earth-based and honoring of the feminine. The training I had received so far had been extremely helpful and enlightening (training I still heavily rely upon and share with others). It was not dishonoring of the feminine or the earth — it simply did not address those areas. I began taking classic Jungian dream symbol and expression classes at The Jung Center, and I taught a few courses at the center as well – starting with a Creative Writing class. I had opened a private hypnotherapy practice and was working on my own feminine journey. My dreams were a large part of the inner work I was doing at the time, leading me to a deeper clarity about the unexplored areas of my psyche for further personal growth. I was actively involved in my life and still awaiting a sign that would lead me toward a new path.

One day I was leaving my office when something on the ground caught my eye, glittering in the sunlight. It was an iridescent sticker of a dragonfly. As I bent down to pick it up, I saw the exact same shape in shadow on the pavement. I looked up and saw a physical dragonfly hovering just above me. Once I recognized what it was, it flew off – message delivered! I knew instantly that this was a meaningful dream symbol (you can receive dream symbols even when you're not asleep) that I needed to follow. In my search for the meaning of this symbol, I was led to the *Medicine Cards*, a book and card set by Jamie Sams and David Carson. I learned about Animal Totems, the medicine they carry, and many teachings from the Native Traditions. These teachings felt familiar and spoke directly to my heart. This was the new path I had been seeking! I began working with and learning from my own team of Animal Totems, which included Dragonfly. Animal Totems are helpers, protectors and guides in the form of creature-beings: the four-leggeds, the creepy-crawlers, the winged ones, and the finned ones. These creature beings each carry a particular medicine or wisdom that can help us physically and spiritually, giving us messages on how to live our lives as Sacred Human Beings. In the Native Traditions, they are viewed as our elder brothers and sisters since they have been on the planet longer than us two-leggeds. As such, they often feel a responsibility to help us along, guiding us in listening to our heart or inner Orenda (that still, small voice of the soul) that is connected to all of Life. The *Sacred Path Cards* and *The Thirteen Original Clan Mothers*, also by Jamie Sams, led me further into the Native Teachings. The *Sacred Path Cards* is another book and card set that covers many of the cherished teachings and ceremonies of the Red Road, incorporating many different viewpoints and tribes from the teachings that Jamie Sams learned from a wide variety of native teachers. *The Thirteen Original Clan Mothers* book presents ancient sacred teachings of the Sisterhood as they relate to the Divine Feminine. So here in three different books by the same author I had found a spiritual path – the Red Road – honoring Mother Earth and the teachings to help me unfold my gifts, talents and abilities as a woman.

Because no one else was teaching this material in Houston at that time (to my knowledge) and because I wanted to continue working with the teachings myself, I began incorporating what I was learning from the Animal Totems, Clan Mothers and Sacred Path information into the classes I was teaching at The Jung Center and into my private hypnotherapy practice, and eventually I formed a monthly Clan Mother Circle for women to come together to explore the teachings of the Sisterhood. The language and information of the Native Teachings touched my heart and resonated deeply within my soul, allowing me to quickly move forward in my spiritual growth. The Teachings were helping me to re-member who I was, reconfiguring my inner landscape in order to expand and deepen my awareness of my place in the Universe.

This material was new to me and the other students. Historically, each Tribe's traditions and ways had been shared from one generation to the next in the Oral Tradition (from mouth to ear), often being passed down in secret. It was only in the 1970s that Native Ceremonies were fully restored to the Native People in the United States, after being outlawed in the late 1800s. I am forever grateful to Jamie Sams and other early, brave native writers like Brooke "Medicine Eagle" Edwards and Ed "Eagle Man" McGaa, who made these teachings available to everyone through their writings – often bearing the displeasure of certain elders for sharing outside of their Tribe and deviating from the Oral Tradition. From these authors, I learned about the Rainbow Tribe – people from all different race and ethnicity backgrounds with different shades of skin tones but red on the inside because of an affinity and resonance with the Native Ways, honoring Mother Earth and All our Relations. If you feel in your heart that you are a member of the Rainbow Tribe, I invite you to seek out these and other writings for a fuller understanding of the myriad and bountiful teachings that comprise Native Spirituality. Fortunately for us, there are many more offerings now than when I began my journey.

I was – and still am – so happy and grateful to be part of the Rainbow Tribe. After being on the Red Road for many years, it was learned from an aged family member through oral family lore that I do carry a native lineage. It has been passed down through my mother's line from the Erie Tribe, also known as the People of the Long Tail which refers to the eastern mountain lion that lived so abundantly on the southern shores of Lake Erie. The Erie were mostly killed off by the Iroquois in the 1650s, and survivors were adopted into other tribes. Some of the descendants of the Erie adopted by the Seneca eventually returned to the Ohio area and were known as the Mingo (aka Ohio Iroquois or Ohio Seneca). This information was volunteered when a great uncle that I had never met learned through other relatives of my interest in the Native Ways. It is simply family lore and cannot be proven one way or another. I feel no need for that – I feel the truth of it for me. Many people I have met on the Red Road, especially where I live now in North Carolina, have some family lore which points to native blood in their lineage. It can't be documented or proven, just like mine cannot, which is perfectly okay. The connection we feel in our hearts to a particular tradition, in the end, is just as powerful as the blood lineage we may carry. I have found that these heart affinities often come from previous lifetimes where the tradition was passed to us through our bloodlines. One Cherokee elder put it succinctly, "If we go back far enough, we are all sitting around the same fire!" Zoe, Rockingbear's wife, when asked if she was part native would sometimes reply with a joke, "Just my right arm from the elbow down!" and she spoke of a t-shirt that said, "I'm part white but I can't prove it" – all to point out the silliness of trying to prove something to someone else. This is not to detract in any way from tribal affiliation and registration or from those who can prove their blood lineage and live their lives in accordance with that lineage. In the winter of 2001, R. Carlos Nakai, the world's premier performer of the Native American flute, played at a benefit concert I attended in Asheville, North Carolina, in support of flute maker Hawk Littlejohn's family, after Hawk Littlejohn's passing. Before starting his song, R. Carlos asked how many in the audience were Native Americans. After many hands shot up, he asked, "And where were the rest of you born?" That earned a good laugh. We are all indigenous beings. Whether we remember that fact and live from our indigenous heart is another story.

We can respectfully incorporate the teachings and wisdom ways of different indigenous, spiritual traditions by skillfully weaving them into our personal spiritual practice. In essence, by exploring the teachings that resonate with our hearts, we are creating our own unique religion — one that continually evolves with us as we deepen our relationship with the Divine. The operative word is *respectfully* – seeking out teachers who have been taught well in the Oral Tradition that calls to us, even to the point of relocating to be near the teacher of our choice. Unbeknownst to me at the time, that's exactly what I did – moving from Houston to Western North Carolina so that I could study with my teacher face to face.

So many of the indigenous teachings are passed down mouth to ear and take time to absorb and fully understand. Rockingbear was asked by several people through the years for permission to write his life story and capture his teachings, but declined each time after much discernment, choosing to honor the Oral Traditions. He was, however, fully open to the idea of a person writing down what they had personally received from his teachings and offering that to the world. This book offers teachings I absorbed from years of sitting with Rockingbear, learning the ceremonies and healing ways he modeled and taught so well, and, in particular, how they relate to calling in a relationship with our Beloved. Rockingbear read the very first, very rough draft of this offering many, many moons ago. He is now in the Spirit World — he dropped his physical robe in January of 2013 – and, with that twinkle in his eye, he is most likely laughing because it has taken me this long to complete what I started so long ago AND he is most definitely holding the wisdom that now is the perfect time to offer these teachings to those seeking to call their Soul Companion to them.

One of the Native teachings that especially resonated with me was about the Dreamtime – a parallel reality beyond space and time – which is also called the Fifth Dimension. It is a web of cosmic light and energy that can be traversed through mind journeys and out-of-body experiences. We naturally travel in the Dreamtime throughout the day – through what we call daydreams, musings or imagination. We can also consciously choose to journey in the Dreamtime to receive information and messages from the Medicine Ancestors, Totems and Spirit Guides. The teachings of the Dreamtime were similar to and completely compatible with the spiritual training I had received earlier in my life so I felt skillful in offering Dreamtime journey experiences to others. These journeys are almost always aided and informed by shamanic drumming. At first I simply played a drumming tape to accompany the class participants on their Dreamtime journeys, never thinking that I would drum myself. Great Spirit and my son had other ideas. At a Pow-Wow and Native Arts and Craft Show in Houston, my 1-year-old son was drawn to a table laden with 2-sided drums made from hollowed tree trunks and wouldn't stop yelling at the top of his lungs when I tried to lead him away. Needless to say, we left with a drum and I started drumming. Having listened to the drumming tapes so many times, I found I was able to maintain the correct rhythm and beat, feeling quite at ease and amazed at how right it felt. There is more than drumming involved in supervising Dreamtime journeys, for which my previous spiritual training had abundantly prepared me. The drummer is also spiritually responsible for the dreamers and must be proficient in guiding them back to the here and now should they get lost in the Cosmos and need help to return.

About a year after I began drumming, the visions of the mountains started and they didn't stop until my decision to move had been made. After we settled into our new home in the Asheville area, I began teaching again, primarily the Clan Mothers Circle with a group of women in Hendersonville, NC. I knew I had been led to the Blue Ridge Mountains for many reasons, one of which was to find my teacher. I was seeking a teacher in the physical, someone in the Native Traditions. So far on this path, my teachers had been my Spirit Helpers, Animal Totems and the Clan Mothers, through the authors of the many helpful books I've already mentioned. I missed the camaraderie I had experienced in the Inner Peace Movement with like-minded spiritual seekers and wondered if I would ever find it again. One of the women in the Clan Mothers Circle told me about a native teacher up in the mountains who held teaching circles. He was having an open house at his lodge that Sunday and did I want to go? I did. We traveled up together as she had been there before and it's a good thing too as the lodge was somewhat hidden away with many twists and turns. This was my first meeting with Will Rockingbear, a Cherokee teacher and healer. I had previously experienced a dreamtime journey with him on the banks of the Swannanoa River in conjunction with an international dream conference but hadn't actually met him. He had a calm demeanor, gentle but strong, and was on the tall side and well-proportioned with blue eyes and a silver-haired ponytail (which later he shaved for a bald head but kept his walrus mustache). He had a presence about him and could ask the most penetrating questions right to the heart of any issue.

He usually carried a twinkle in his blue eyes, and he had a wicked, dry sense of humor. After one talk at an Asheville church, one of his students approached him saying that a woman wanted to meet him but she felt afraid of him. He told the student to bring her over. She reiterated that she felt afraid of him and he replied, "You don't even know me. You must have me confused with someone else." She thought about it for a bit and answered, "You're right and I know who it is. Thank you. I'm not afraid of you any longer." And she walked away. Another woman, several years later, approached him after a teaching circle and said to him, "Rockingbear, the way you say some things, I can't tell when you are joking and when you're serious" and he replied earnestly but facetiously, "I'm always serious." She nodded and said, "Okay, that makes it easier, thank you," totally believing he was serious. When this story was related to me, I had a good chuckle as it really was hard sometimes to tell the difference with his deadpan delivery.

He was an excellent joke teller. He used humor to talk about serious and important teachings as he never preached or judged. He taught through stories — some poignant, some hilarious, some so close to home you wanted to wriggle away from the teaching, and he always reminded us to experience the joy in life and give gratitude, lots of gratitude.

I listened intently to his teachings that afternoon at the open house. He ended by drumming for us while we journeyed into the invisible world of the Dreamtime. In my journey, I saw a pod of Orca whales swimming down the valley, totally at home in the mountains — such a wondrous and beautiful sight with the blue shimmering mountains all around them! When I asked them, "What are you doing here?" they replied, "We have been here for a very long time, since the time when these oldest mountains on earth were surrounded by the ocean waters. We asked the mountains to call you back as this is your home. You have finally returned home. We will help you – all you have to do is ask for assistance." I was crying by the end of the journey and completely filled in a way that I had never before experienced. When Rockingbear shared with the group that there was room in his teaching circles for those who wanted to make a weekly commitment, I instantly knew that I wanted to study with him and continue my training with him as my teacher. The next week I joined the Monday Night Circle and continued sitting in circle with Rockingbear for over 15 years.

Rockingbear was a tremendous healing force in my life. His gentle vibration held the most balanced energy between the masculine and feminine natures of anyone I had met. Learning from his wisdom and being around his keen discerning abilities was deeply healing for me – letting go of the hurts, pain and sorrow held from my past experiences, with men in general and in relationship, and personally and collectively held in the pain body spoken of so eloquently by Eckhart Tolle. Through Rockingbear's teachings, I experienced a deep purification and self-realization about the wounded, hurt pieces of my heart and psyche. I was still fragile when I began sitting in circle with Rockingbear, not completely sure of myself on this new path. I was a single mother, supporting my son and myself through legal secretarial work, work that I did competently but not wholeheartedly. I had been bruised by my experience in the corporate world, finding it de-humanizing and mechanistic. I didn't trust myself or believe in myself as I had when I was younger. I was lonely and had many issues I needed to heal in regards to intimate relationships. Rockingbear and the other healers in the Monday Night Circle saw me and accepted me for who I really was – a healer and a spiritual teacher – and with their support and encouragement, I began to blossom and cultivate my personal power to a greater degree. What I saw in Rockingbear – an impeccable teacher who was loving and gentle, discerning and honest – healed the cynicism and despair I had built up as a shield around my heart. The authentic, loving connection I saw between Rockingbear and his wife Zoe gave me hope that it was possible to stay in my power AND be in an intimate relationship at the same time. Also, the teachings shared in *The Thirteen Original Clan Mothers* helped me immensely. I realized that what I had experienced in the past with relationships was based on social expectations, distortions, and fears. I wanted more than that and now I could see a good example of it right before my eyes, and every week it was slowly helping to heal the wounds I carried about myself as a woman and whether I could sustain a healthy relationship. I was ready to invite a man into my life as my partner, to experience the spiritual growth that comes from being in an intimate, heart-connected relationship. It was time for the Calling Ceremony!

Doing my Calling Ceremony was the culmination of months and years of preparation – the spiritual foundation I had received from the Inner Peace Movement, the inner healing work I had done on my Feminine Journey in Houston, and now more inner scrutiny and transformation with the help of Rockingbear, to be ready for what I wanted – an authentic, intimate, loving, monogamous, long-term relationship with a physical man. Do you see how precise and exact the wording was for what I wanted? I sweated buckets, focusing my desires, wants, goals and intentions until those specific words were born from my heart and soul, pinpointing my complete intention in this area of my life. This ceremony was one more of the many actions I needed to take to physically manifest my heart's desire for a Soul Companion. I was calling to this man, my Beloved, my partner, my mate, my husband, whom I hadn't met yet physically but with whom I so deeply wanted to make a connection. I had been yearning for my Other to come into my life for a very long time and I was finally ready to set down the fears and doubts that had assailed me, to focus my intentions and to co-create with Great Spirit what I wanted in my life.

As I sat cross-legged in front of the Fire, I looked at the items on the small cloth altar beside me – a feather, a stone, a picture of myself and my son, and a dragonfly carved from crystal and silver. All these items held deep significance for me, showing the true energetic workings of my inner and outer life. Rockingbear was behind me playing the large, deep-voiced Tarahumara Drum, then to the left side, then to the right, in front, above my head, low to the floor, and then again behind, repeating this pattern again and again, creating a resonating sphere of energy around me to magnetize and send out the intentions held in my heart. The drum beat alerted all my Spirit Helpers and Medicine Ancestors and the Spirit Helpers and Medicine Ancestors of the man coming into my life to hear my intentions and lend assistance in creating the connection that would draw us together. I was calling my Soul Companion to me, to come into my life in a good way, to know who I was and what I wanted in this sacred relationship. I was setting my personal and relationship boundaries, communicating my heart's desires and opening myself to his presence and energy.

While the drum continued its strong, hypnotic beat, my everyday thoughts fled, pounded away by the drum's stream of pure energy and leaving only my heart's desires and intentions in my consciousness. I could no longer hold the thoughts in my brain of the mantra that I had been intoning in the weeks before the ceremony, "I am ready for an intimate, authentic relationship with my Soul Companion." Now I was simply being this specific want, this clarified desire. Sandwiched between the drumming and the Fire, I began to grow very warm. Rockingbear had placed a medicine blanket around my shoulders, enveloping me in a soft, protective cocoon. Sweat trickled down the sides of my body beneath my clothes. The heat and pounding of the drum created so much energy, such a loud intention, that I seemed to be crackling with the intensity of the building energy. It was so very powerful, yet calming and peaceful. I was almost floating while at the same time I felt the energy of Turtle close to me, connecting me to Mother Earth and her teachings of only being able to move forward in life, unable to go backward. I welcomed Turtle's assistance with my Calling.

Eventually, Rockingbear instructed me to go through the Fire and sit on the other side to better see myself. Still feeling the tremendous heat and light, not only from the Fire and the drum, but now also from the sun, I realized I was seeing a beach with endless sand and water in the distance. I was pulled there, the waves of the ocean further magnetizing my thoughts and feelings. I could not see my partner in clear detail when I was asked to, but

I was aware of his presence. I talked with him, welcoming him into my life and my heart. I expressed my gratitude that he and I would soon be together physically, able to touch each other. I gave him a macaw feather as my troth to him. He gave me a wolf skin and a white flower as his pledge to me in return. I clearly saw the gifts given and received in every detail. I told him where I lived – in Asheville, Western North Carolina – and the places I most frequented so he could easily find me. The vision faded, the drumming stopped and Rockingbear said, "It is done." My Soul Companion had been called, he answered, and we had chosen one another. I had called to my Beloved. I had made space in my life for him. I had made spiritual contact with him through the Fire and was now ready and open to welcome my Beloved into my physical life as I had already welcomed him into my heart.

After we were finished, I felt revitalized and was humming with joy and happiness. It seemed as if he were right around the corner. I was prepared to be alert, discerning and in my gratitude. I was confident I would not miss him and he would not miss me. The connection had been made and I felt it already. Several weeks earlier I had awakened from a light sleep to see a pair of gentle, compassionate, brown eyes gazing at me. I felt perfectly safe and cherished by those eyes, and I knew I would be seeing them in person in the near future. I sensed that within one year we would meet. I had waited for so long that I could be patient for a little while longer. I knew the vibration of the one coming into my life. I knew most of his qualities. I realized that I really, truly already did know him in a very deep, intimate way because of the Calling Ceremony. This gave me confidence that I would not be meeting a stranger, but someone with whom I had already forged a connection. I was excited, frightened, filled with hope and joy, and grateful for all the forces in the Universe that were mobilizing to assist me in this request I had humbly and with great sincerity put before Great Spirit.

To end any suspense that you may be harboring, I did in fact meet my Soul Companion 10 months after doing the Calling Ceremony through a series of serendipitous events (of course) which I'll share in more detail later in the book, leading to an intimate, authentic, deeply heart-connected relationship. As of this writing, we have been together for 16 years, riding the ups and downs found in any relationship, learning from each other, helping each other to become ever more skillful, authentic and loving. We come from different traditions, different cultures, but the essence of all truth teachings are ultimately the same, enabling us to compliment and support one another (and sometimes drive each other crazy!) on our spiritual journeys.

The whole purpose of being in relationship is to heal each other, with compassion and gentleness, not cruelty and hardness. Being in this type of relationship has opened many doors for me, helping me to more fully do what I came to do, and healing me in ways I had never imagined. As I continued my apprenticeship with Rockingbear, learning the Soul Retrieval Ceremony and many other healing ceremonies, opening my own Medicine Lodge, and sharing with others about my experience of calling my Soul Companion, I began to train for the Calling Ceremony. Through my work with this ceremony over many years, I have been led to share the following teachings so you too may manifest your heart's desire for a heart-connected relationship with your Soul Companion. Many of the ideas and teachings presented here you can do by yourself, but if you have access to a spiritual teacher or a Medicine Healer who can help you, so much the better.

We all need teachers in our lives so we can learn what we don't know we don't know. When we know what we don't know, it's easy to find it, but it's often what we don't know we don't know that makes the crucial difference. Because of our ignorance about our true identity as spiritual beings – beings of light and energy that cannot be created nor destroyed – and the sacred teachings that remind us of these truths, we have often experienced more pain, suffering and sorrow than was necessary. Through greater understanding of who we are, what we have come to do and how to do it, we can truly live our lives with grace and ease, learning what we need to learn without such great suffering and despair. My teachers tell me that we are here to be happy, that our purpose is to be happy – not surface happy by having all the modern toys and comforts, but truly deep-down-in-the-very-fiber-of-our-being happy—feeling limitless joy and gratitude even amongst the challenges, pain and grief we experience in life. Be brave, very brave, if you too want to be in relationship with your Soul Companion, as this is dangerous work we do here – you may just end up being happy!

Is the Calling Ceremony for You?

Are you ready to embark on a journey of personal power – a journey where the twists and turns remain to be seen but the final destination is clear? If so, I ask that you start by considering some questions to see if you are willing and ready to begin the Calling Ceremony for your Soul Companion. When you can answer yes to each of these questions, you have already taken the first steps on this journey. These questions will give you an idea of the inner work and self-reflection needed in order to be clear about who you perceive yourself to be and who you are calling into your life to be in relationship with you. Only then will you be ready to do the inner clearing and preparation needed in order to sit before the Fire and make the calling for your Soul Companion. Although this journey into your self-realization and sacred partnership can be arduous, I can't think of a more fulfilling quest – to heal yourself and to continue evolving spiritually while being in an intimate, authentic relationship with your Soul Companion.

These questions will also help you define for yourself what you mean by the words Soul Companion, rather than using boyfriend, partner or spouse. A Soul Companion can be some or all of these labels but with the added spiritual connection and awareness of that incredibly deep heart connection that will help sustain you on your spiritual journey. Being in relationship with your Soul Companion helps you do what you have come to Planet Earth to do, not necessarily through overt actions by your Soul Companion, but rather by their unconditional love and support, and the clear reflection and impeccability that's needed to be in relationship with them.

Occasionally, after looking at these questions, an individual will realize that what they really want is someone to take care of them – emotionally, physically or financially – or someone who is only in their life when it's convenient for sexual release, or simply a companion to go out with occasionally for movies or dinner to alleviate loneliness or boredom. The inner work required for this ceremony may be viewed as too scary, time consuming or simply not necessary. While there is nothing wrong with these types of relationships, they are not congruent with being in relationship with a Soul Companion, therefore the Calling Ceremony would not be appropriate or warranted. The Calling Ceremony is based on a willingness to be in a sacred partnership of the heart and soul, one that transcends relationships based solely on physical beauty, the size of financial assets, social standing or prestige.

Are you truly looking for a Soul Companion, and if so, is now the time in your life to do this Ceremony? Please take your time reflecting on the following questions. An initial response may not stand up to your inner scrutiny. You may feel some shifts occurring just by asking yourself these questions. If the answer to a question is no, go within to see if you are willing to make the necessary changes in your thoughts, words or actions. If so, make a new agreement. These changes don't have to be a process. As soon as we receive the insight, we can make a new agreement and live our life differently. If the answer is still no, then consider that the Calling Ceremony is not right for you at this time.

Notice, each question is framed with the words, "Are you willing?" It doesn't mean that you are perfect at it – otherwise no one would ever begin the ceremony! By being willing you are agreeing to do your best in each of these areas, to be as clear as you can be and to be open to further clarity. Each step of your journey has been completed because you were willing to take that step in the first place and then willing to take the next step and the next. Now, find a quiet place within you, take several deep breaths and allow your consciousness to drop into your inner sacred space to contemplate more fully these queries.

1. *Am I willing to stretch myself, to go beyond my unexamined beliefs to discover more fully my truths?*

2. *Am I willing to be honest with myself – my feelings, thoughts and emotions?*

3. *Am I willing to ferret out my fears and release them back to the wild?*

4. *Am I willing to respect and honor myself as I look at the habit patterns and agreements that no longer serve me and make the changes I need to make?*

5. *Am I willing to take the actions or non-actions I need to take in my life to be ready for my Soul Companion?*

6. *Am I willing to clear the clutter from my life, physically, emotionally and spiritually, to become more clear and light?*

7. *Am I willing to create space and time in my life for my Soul Companion so he or she doesn't have to push or elbow his or her way into my life?*

8. *Am I willing to be authentic, honest, powerful, vulnerable, open-hearted and intimate in this ceremony and with my Soul Companion?*

9. *Am I willing to be patient; trusting in Great Spirit and Divine Timing so I can be in the right place at the right time to physically meet my Soul Companion?*

10. *Am I willing to listen to my heart – my Orenda – and to Great Spirit to truly hear and trust the messages that will guide me in this ceremony?*

11. *Am I willing to co-create my life with Great Spirit, taking responsibility for my happiness and well-being, so that I no longer live my life from powerlessness or the role of the victim?*

12. *Am I willing to do whatever I need to do or not do in my life in order to call my Soul Companion to me so we can be in relationship with one another?*

When you can answer a resounding yes to each of these questions, then you are ready to approach the East Door of the Medicine Wheel for the Calling Ceremony. You are now ready to begin with grace and ease, with your whole heart and soul.

Is it an inner workout? Yes. Are you going to use all of you – your blood, sweat and tears? Of course. Are you fearful? Probably! Excited? Absolutely! So let's begin.

HOW TO WORK WITH THIS BOOK

In the Native Traditions, all of life is organized and experienced through the teachings of the Medicine Wheel – a circle with no beginning and no end, a never-ending spiral. This circular worldview creates a non-linear way of looking at and interacting with the world and all the lessons we learn as we journey through life. Each direction on the Medicine Wheel offers its own teaching, insights and wisdom, varying to some degree depending on which native or earth-based tradition you consult. The Medicine Wheel shows us an energetic way of moving through life which acknowledges the Rites of Passage we all experience – birth, growth, death, and rebirth.

Traditionally, there are Seven Sacred Directions. In addition to the four cardinal directions of East, North, West and South, there is also Above, Below and Within. You can picture all seven of these directions as compass points offering a 3-dimensional point of view of where we are at any given point in our lives. There is a huge body of knowledge held by the different native traditions regarding the Sacred Directions, the Medicine Wheel and the act of Calling in the Directions and I encourage you to seek this information. The following is only a small snapshot, offered to give you a basic understanding and get you started.

In the Cherokee tradition, we start in the East, progressing around the wheel counter-clockwise. The East Direction is the place of new beginnings, sunrise, far vision, solar energy and the divine masculine. Illumination, Clarity and Beginner's Mind are the powers offered by the teachings of the East.

Then we progress to the North Direction – the place of the white-haired ones or elders, the white-furred ones, and ancient wisdom and ceremonies passed down through the ages. Gratitude, Prayer and Abundance are the powers held in the North.

On to the West Direction – that place of sunset, the time in between or twilight, lunar energies and the divine feminine. Introspection (going within for answers) and Alignment with the Inner and Outer Cycles of Life are the powers of the West.

The South Direction is the place of healing, medicinal plants, the divine child and opportunities for growth. Childlike Innocence, Faith and Trust, along with Laughter are the powers held in the South.

The Above Direction is the place of the Starry Medicine Bowl, the Sky Nation, and the limitlessness and vastness of the Dreamtime – that place beyond time and space, also called the 5th Dimension. Imagination, Dreams and One-Mindedness are the powers that reside in the Sky Nation.

The Below Direction is the place of Mother Earth (Pacha Mama) and all the children of the Earth Blanket – the elements, minerals, stone people, tree people (standing ones), plant people, creepy-crawlers, finned ones, winged ones and the four-leggeds, to name just a few. Nourishment on every level, appreciation of Diversity and the Beauty of Life are the powers held so sweetly by Pacha Mama.

The Within Direction supports our inner sacred space – the inner landscape of our soul identity that informs and creates everything in our life, and our unbreakable connection to the Seven Generations who came before us and the Seven Generations that come after us. Wise Choices, Discernment, Purpose and Protection are the powers residing in this place where we connect with and honor the Medicine Ancestors.

When I asked my Spirit Guides for the best way to present the teachings for this Calling Ceremony, I was shown the Medicine

Wheel. In positioning the teachings on the Wheel, a way is created for you to easily move through the teachings and work presented in each of the seven directions, in your own timing and often in your own way. Instead of a linear configuration, the circular Medicine Wheel invites you to return again and again to certain teachings, as many times as you need – rather like spinning a web or creating a multi-faceted geometric shape. This circular journey invokes your heart and your inner soul voice – the Orenda – allowing the Orenda to guide you on the journey of calling to your Soul Companion.

Whenever we begin Ceremony or sit in circle, we call in the Seven Sacred Directions by addressing the Spirit Keepers that reside in each direction – paying homage and voicing gratitude for the medicine and power held in each direction – and asking each Spirit Keeper for assistance with our endeavors. When the Directions are called, it is a calling from the heart – just like this ceremony – without a set script or rote prayer. In this way we keep our relationship alive with each member of the Planetary Family – recognized as equal to us two-leggeds and to one another – fully interconnected and interdependent on the Wheel of Life. As you navigate through the preparation, practices and teachings presented in each direction, your unique and individual calling ceremony will take shape, held within the sacred hoop of the Medicine Wheel, often called the Web of Life, with all its power and wisdom.

The following poem, *Walking the Beauty Way*, is offered as a prayer of intention, a blessing for the journey upon which you are embarking – calling your Soul Companion to you with grace and ease through an indigenous-based tradition and ceremony as I learned it from my teacher, Will Rockingbear.

Walking the Beauty Way

My eyes are open, Creator
I see the beauty in every person I meet
as I walk the Beauty Way

My ears are listening, Creator
I hear the words of Wisdom and Truth
as I walk the Beauty Way

My lips are moving, Creator
I speak round, soft words of encouragement
as I walk the Beauty Way

My voice is singing, Creator
I share a song of joy and gratitude
as I walk the Beauty Way

My hands are open, Creator
I receive the gifts of abundance life offers me
as I walk the Beauty Way

My heart is tender, Creator
I am generous in expressing my love
as I walk the Beauty Way

My stomach is full, Creator
I am fed by the stories of my Ancestors
as I walk the Beauty Way

My feet are moving me forward, Creator
I tread gently on Mother Earth
as I walk the Beauty Way

My body is strong and supple, Creator
I do my work with grace and ease
as I walk the Beauty Way

My spirit is soaring among the stars, Creator
I dream and envision a peace-filled life
as I walk the Beauty Way

My entire Being is awake and alive, Creator
I honor my connection to the Web of Life
as I walk the Beauty Way

Robin White Star
Vision Quest 2009
The Year of Living in Peace

East Direction

CLARITY TO BEGIN

———∘————————————∘———

"All you SpiritKeepers of the East, Come, Look this way!
We give gratitude for this new beginning, for the clarity of
mind and openness of heart to learn and grow.

Thank you, Eagle, Condor and Hawk – you high flying ones –
for your gifts of insight and ability to look
at our lives with a benevolent eye.

Thank you for this new day, this opportunity
for beginner's mind, to truly experience
the joy and humbleness of starting anew.

Thank you, Divine Masculinity, that solar energy and
power of protection, be with us as we begin this journey"
Wah Doh

What is the Calling Ceremony?

The Calling Ceremony unleashes and activates the powers of clear intention, specificity without limitations, willingness to receive, manifestation, magnetization, and gratitude. All these strands create a complex matrix, weaving an energetic web composed of your heart's desire and clarity of mind. If you just want to be wishful, vague, limiting in your request or complaining about your current situation, then this ceremony is not for you. When your thoughts, words and actions are aligned and congruent, there is no way NOT to receive that which you request. In fact, the most alarming part of the ceremony is that you will receive **exactly** what you are asking for. That's why it's so important to be clear and to do the work you need to do on yourself to remove the fears, doubts, limitations, prejudices, and beliefs that have been blocking you from being who you really are. Being willing to make the transformations in your own life, whether or not the relationship you are calling has yet manifested in the physical, is part of the magnetization of the calling. How many times have you thought that if you already had the relationship you deeply desire, then it would be simple to make the changes in your life in order to keep it? It doesn't work that way.

Like attracts like in the Invisible, Intangible World. You must become, to the best of your ability, the person you wish to attract – not in every instance and nuance but in the basic resonance. For example, if you wish to be with a partner who is financially responsible, you need to make sure that your finances are in good shape and that no matter how much income is involved you are being responsible with it. If it's important to you that your partner is fit and trim, then you have to look at your own level of health and fitness. You won't necessarily be on the same level of development as the partner you are calling, but the vibration must be there to have a resonance between you. The adjustments may be small. As you discern who you perceive yourself to be and the qualities you want in your Soul Companion, you may find that new urges and desires arise to grow, shed, and transform certain qualities, habits, attitudes, and actions you are currently manifesting in your life. You will begin to see whether what you are asking for in your partner is congruent with how you are willing to live your life.

This ceremony requires a degree of honest self-reflection in order for you to truly call your Soul Companion to you. By qualifying your calling for a Soul Companion, you are invoking the clearest, purest and highest form of relationship you can envision (it will be different for each one of you – there is no one highest form!) so it's not a surprise that you are required to be the clearest, purest and highest form of yourself in order to do this calling. If your idea of an intimate, authentic relationship involves having someone take care of you, or taking advantage of someone, or taking more than you are willing to give, or giving more than you are willing to receive, then it is unlikely that you will call a Soul Companion to you. The heart connection and deep love between Soul Companions excludes this type of manipulation, dysfunction and disharmony that comes from living life solely from the social self. The social self or the small self is impregnated with the dogma of rights and wrongs, do's and don'ts, and domesticated to the point where there is little self-understanding, self-reflection or alignment with your inner spiritual truths. Your work is to uncover the illusions that keep you on the hamster wheel of judgment, comparison, competition, status quo and blind obedience to social mores and norms.

All of the inner work of self-assessment – healing of your past wounds, examination of your beliefs and replacement with your truths, owning your power, claiming your divine right to be in a loving, authentic relationship – is also applicable if you are currently in a relationship. The Calling Ceremony, once begun, never ends. The essence of your spiritual evolution is to continue calling your life into being. Calling for a Soul Companion and calling for your current relationship to be more soulful and heart-centered are actually one and the same. There are natural cycles within any sacred relationship that mirror our own cycles of self-discovery, our dying to the outmoded ways of being, and rising new and fresh like the phoenix, declaring ourselves reborn. We then have the opportunity to choose each other all over again, restating our commitments and agreements with our Beloved. Or, if we so choose, we can end the relationship with impeccability, gratitude and a clear sense of the healing that has taken place, creating space for another Beloved to come into our lives for the next part of our journey.

The Calling Ceremony demands that you see yourself as you truly are – a spiritual being that has a physical body, not a physical body that has a soul or spiritual spark somewhere inside. Just this change in perspective will make all the difference as to how you live your life, make your choices and move beyond the social imprints of fear and limitation that come from thinking of yourself as only a physical being. As a spiritual being wearing a physical body at this time, you are the sum total of every experience you have had throughout eons of time. Think of the knowledge, wisdom and vastness that are the real you! By moving your understanding of yourself from a physical being to a spiritual being, you can begin to take responsibility for your life and co-create your life with Great Spirit, dreaming a new reality for yourself and the world. This is the power of the Calling Ceremony.

WHO IS A SOUL COMPANION?

My teachers tell me that the purpose of being in relationship is to heal each other. An intimate relationship with another can create this healing dynamic, whether we are calling a man, a woman or a person of non-binary gender to come into our life as a Soul Companion. The Mayan say, "You are another myself." When we look deeply into the eyes of *another myself* we can see ourselves more clearly. The nature of an intimate, authentic relationship asks that we become mirrors for each other. And if we cannot see what is in the mirror, we are asked to hold up a lantern for each other so we can more clearly see those parts of ourselves that are in shadow, that require more light – turning the lantern this way and that way – so those parts can be recognized, reconciled and integrated. That is what we do with a Soul Companion. We heal each other. We are in relationship with our Soul Companion to help each other on this journey of self-discovery, self-understanding and self-realization.

We can do this mirroring for each other with great love, compassion, gentleness, humor, respect, intimacy, trust and equality. We can use round, soft words when we need to express our truths, words that we don't need to regret or apologize for later. We can be truly vulnerable with our Soul Companion because the level of trust, respect and integrity is high, giving us the knowing that we are safe and cherished. Lies or half-truths are not needed to protect ourselves because we know that the truths we share will not be used against us. Being open-hearted – willing to listen with our hearts so we can completely hear what our partner is saying – heals us and heals our Beloved. Love and compassion are not feelings. They are actions. Although the love we feel for another is pleasant and perhaps even thrilling for us, it doesn't mean a thing to the other person unless we express it through our words, thoughts and actions. Even just saying "I love you" doesn't really mean anything to the other person unless we have congruent actions to express that love. The sentiment of love can be expressed through the soft caress of our eyes, conveyed with a heartfelt hug, or sharing a touch on the shoulder of our Beloved as we pass through the room – so many ways to express love through simple actions. That's why we need to listen to our partner's actions, not their words. Actions tell us when we are in a truly loving relationship. Then our healing can be experienced with joy and happiness, and with grace and ease.

We also have the choice to do this mirroring for each other in hurtful, vengeful, harsh, critical, non-trusting ways, using sharp, pointed words that wound and maim. This leads to withdrawal, shutting down, lashing out, recriminations, jealousy, comparisons, competition and ultimately hatred. Just as a cornered, scared animal will bite and attack to defend itself, we become defensive and attacking when we are fearful and hurt. We become separated from each other because fear already separates us from our true nature – a Sacred Human Being. The healing will still take place because the intensity of the pain, sorrow, and grief eventually carries us to a place where we are willing to make different choices about the actions we need to take and the changes we have been resisting so that we can stop hurting. The tears that fall are important – they cleanse our internal emotional wounds so they don't become septic. Taking these sacred healing tears back inside oneself or *eating our tears* is extremely healing. Instead of blotting them up with a tissue, wiping them away – or, worse yet, stopping the tears altogether – allow them to run into your mouth or gently take a finger to scoop them up and deposit them back into your mouth. This completes the cycle, receiving the endorphins and healing properties from our saltwater tears to transmute the pain and grief into wisdom and love.

We usually experience all these ways at different times in our lives. Whatever way the mirror is held up for us, it gives us the opportunity to learn, grow and heal. One way is through love and compassion, the other through fear and violence. But both ways are teachers. As we evolve on our spiritual journey, we can more fully stand in our personal power with gentle strength, kindness and humility, with love for ourselves and others. When we feel worthy of love and respect, we will naturally choose – through synchronicity – people and events that mirror back love and respect to us. When we feel unworthy of love and respect, we will naturally choose – again through synchronicity – people and events that mirror back that lack of love and respect to us. It starts with our inner reality and moves outward into our interactions with life. This is the way we change the world, by changing our inner reality. We can experience life with grace and ease – it is a choice of staying awake, aware and intentional on our journey, opening our hearts to joy and happiness.

Rockingbear taught me that pain is a natural part of life here in the physical, that there is no escaping the pain of loss and heartbreak or physical pain; however, suffering is optional! Suffering comes from the mind – the ego – holding on to the pain. Of course we need our ego to help us navigate in this complex world, but it certainly doesn't need to be in the driver's seat, steering with the fears and limitations that keep us separated from our true self. When we realize that all the pain, grief and trauma in our lives has given us the gift of who we are right now, we can give thanks for all our experiences and for all the people in our lives who taught us along the way, and then let go of the past with deep gratitude and respect. Otherwise we will continue to suffer, coloring our perceptions of what is by living in the past, limiting our choices and creating a stuck place within us. Let go of regret! Rockingbear shared that he was amazed when someone felt badly about themselves for needing to go through a learning experience (sometimes again and again) and calling themselves names – stupid, slow, bad – as if they weren't supposed to ever, ever make a mistake. He said that these violent acts of self-judgment, shame and regret have an awful smell and are toxic and acidic to the soul.

One time, after a particularly virulent attack on myself for some perceived mistake on my part, my Spirit Guides shared quite unequivocally and emphatically with me, "No one is counting how many times you fall down – we aren't counting, no one is counting! All we do is notice when you get back up because then we can walk beside you again." As I digested this teaching, it occurred to me that I never counted how many times my son fell down while he was learning to stand, walk and run. The same is true of Great Spirit – Great Spirit is there to show us the next step, not criticize how long it takes us to master the step we are on. This teaching has been central to my ability to truly learn from life's lessons and to continually let go of the judgments that could keep me stuck in regret and shame. I no longer use the word "mistake" when describing my experiences. Instead, I refer to the experience as a "learning lesson" or a "stepping stone." I find this more accurately names the truth of what is occurring in my life and helps remind me not to be violent and harsh with myself.

With this understanding, we step off the merry-go-round of playing the victim (poor little me), the perpetrator (judging ourselves) and the rescuer (self-medicating). Once we no longer need to play these roles within ourselves, we find that, magically, others stop playing these roles in our lives and stop asking us to play these roles in their lives. We become more real, authentic and responsive to our inner truths, and act accordingly with self-acceptance, love and compassion. This is the freedom of the soul – the freedom found from being in relationship with another who is seeking this same level of spiritual understanding and enlightenment.

We cannot call our Soul Companion from a place of being stuck. It's just not possible. From a place of inner gratitude for and freedom from the past, we can be clear enough to send out our calling, our yearning, our heart's desire, our total commitment to co-creating a beautiful, intimate, authentic relationship based on love and compassion, understanding and wisdom. It doesn't mean that we don't still have lessons to learn and levels of enlightenment to master, but we can do so without the feelings of self-hatred, guilt, and remorse and without inflicting punishment upon ourselves and our loved ones. In our heart of hearts we carry the acorn of knowledge of how to be in an empowering relationship with our Beloved. We innately know how to learn and love with grace and ease. It's time to reclaim this wisdom.

OVERVIEW OF THE CALLING CEREMONY

The Calling Ceremony, as set down on these pages, has 3 major parts: (1) requesting the Calling Ceremony and wholeheartedly engaging in the inner healing work to be done; (2) sitting with the Fire to energetically connect with your Soul Companion; and (3) staying in your gratitude and paying attention to the ongoing signs and messages from Great Spirit in order to physically meet your Soul Companion. By requesting this ceremony, you are informing every being in the Universe that you are willing to take the actions and non-actions needed to transcend old, limiting beliefs, to transform your life with the power of gratitude and seek purity and clarity with your intentions. This work may involve requesting other ceremonies and healings to assist you as you do the necessary internal work before sitting with the Fire. These ceremonies and healing ways are detailed in the North Direction.

The preparation involves (1) doing a series of self-reflection exercises where you look at yourself with an observant, loving eye to see who you truly perceive yourself to be. Some of this work entails journaling or listing the fears, beliefs, prejudices, and limitations that have been holding you hostage; (2) discerning and putting exact words to what type of relationship you wish to call into your life; (3) creating a home altar to honor all the Beings who are assisting you in calling your Beloved and to serve as a touchstone during the entire ceremony; and (4) creating a current list or account of detailed attributes you desire in your Soul Companion and also of those attributes or qualities that are not acceptable.

When your preparation is complete, you then sit with the Sacred Fire, and with the Medicine Healer who has been working with you in your preparation. The Medicine Healer's energy assists you, adding strength to your request so that your invitation has the highest and deepest possible resonance. After you have connected energetically with your Soul Companion through the Fire, your work is to listen and trust, be open and receptive, and stay in a place of gratitude so you can be in the right place at the right time to make the physical connection. Then you allow the intimacy and authenticity between you to naturally unfold – getting to know one another in this time and place – until you absolutely know and accept that indeed this is your Soul Companion.

What you experience and learn through your Calling Ceremony will give you the understanding and strength to live your truth and stand in your power, not only in your relationship with your Soul Companion but in every relationship in your life. By learning to take responsibility for your own happiness, fulfillment, joy and abundance, your life becomes a blessing – feeding the Holy and giving back to Great Spirit. Your happiness, joy and healing will radiate or ripple out, touching your Beloved, your family and the world. Others will be inspired by your magic as they see you living in sacred partnership. In this way, you become more fully a Sacred Human Being.

CEREMONY BEGINS WHEN REQUESTED

As soon as you request ceremony, it begins. Whether it takes you a year to complete the preparation or a month, you are in ceremony for the entire time. It's not just when you are sitting in front of the Fire with the Medicine Healer drumming for you that you are in Ceremony. Knowing this, you become more aware, paying attention to what comes into your life – perhaps through dreams, encounters with animals, conversations or books.

Once requested and participated in, ceremony never ends. That is why there are sacred spaces, holy places, on the planet where ceremonies have been held and experienced, and their reverberations are still felt today in those places. Ceremony becomes part of the energetic web, aura or energy pattern available to you for your life. The meaningful and sacred experiences we call rituals and ceremonies become your depth, richness, and spiritual wealth, available to you in times of stress, trauma or illness. As more encounters with ceremony enter your life, you learn how to live in ceremony all the time – like praying without ceasing. Rather than living in the mundane and occasionally visiting the sacred, or living in the sacred and visiting the mundane when necessity requires, you begin to realize that each moment is both, and the mundane and the sacred encompass all states of consciousness. My teachers tell me that living our life as Sacred Human Beings means that each time our heart beats we are in ceremony. No special place, protocol, ritual, or clothing is needed, simply being in a balanced state of consciousness with every heartbeat. We become the Ceremony. Then when we become masters of living in ceremony during every heartbeat, we expand into the spaces *between* the heartbeats! Living in a state of ceremony becomes who we are –

connected, centered, clear and impeccable, remembering who we are and living our life to the fullest of what we are capable of each and every moment. We will still make mistakes (which simply equals "more information") but we will be conscious, intentional, and learning from our experiences. It means being engaged with life, willing to take risks and take responsibility, willing to acknowledge that we are connected to the Web of Life, connected to every sentient being in the Universe and alive with love and compassion for ourselves and others. Love and compassion aren't simply feelings, they are the actions and non-actions we choose to live by. These actions support the truth that we are way bigger than the illusions and limitations that arise from thinking we are only a physical being, disconnected from Divine Source (except for a few moments here and there). Living in a state of ceremony means we are awake and aware of our spiritual nature. Living in a state of ceremony is remembering that we exist in two worlds at the same time – the invisible, intangible world of Great Spirit and the visible, tangible physical world. We are Beings of Light – pure energy that cannot be created or destroyed – eternally connected to and one with Divine Source.

TRADITIONAL WAY OF REQUESTING CEREMONY

In the traditional way, you request a ceremony or teaching by taking the Medicine Healer a bundle of tobacco and asking the Healer to consider your request. This tobacco bundle is usually made from a square piece of red cloth made of cotton or other natural fiber and torn, not cut with scissors (to honor our native ancestors who did not have scissors until after the Western influence). The cloth is then filled with a small pinch of tobacco and tied into a bundle with another piece of red cloth that's been torn into a strip. I have seen many different colors and types of tobacco bundles offered, some with a feather, pinecone or other adornment stuck in the tie. Sometimes an entire package of American Spirit, a Native American ceremonial tobacco, or other specially prepared tobacco offering is wrapped and presented.

When I first gave tobacco to my teacher along with my request, I hadn't asked for any instructions ahead of time so I just handed him an unwrapped package of Red Man chewing tobacco! He graciously accepted it, knowing that I didn't know any better at the time, and without comment. The intention and purity of heart behind the request is just as important – or more important – as the form of your tobacco offering. But it's also appropriate to be as respectful and honoring of the ways of the Medicine Healer as you know to be. It's also okay to ask them directly for teachings on how to be respectful of their traditions. The form in which you ultimately make your bundle is up to you and your inner Orenda or heart-voice. When you are putting together your bundle, intentionally add your prayers and gratitude regarding your request into the bundle with the tobacco.

Original tobacco is a sacred Medicine Plant in the Native ways. It has been used in ceremony since ancient times and has many healing properties, both physical and spiritual. When used without ceremony or ceremonial intent and grown with profit and addiction as its main considerations, it becomes profane and today many suffer the damaging effects from how it is commercially grown and manufactured and from how they are using it in their lives. Everything in nature carries its own medicine. Our task is to learn about the medicine and use it appropriately. This is the way we honor the diversity of life and all the different medicines available to us.

I used to be very prejudiced against tobacco, not realizing that it is a powerful healing tool that has been misused and abused. Initially I didn't even want to visit relatives in Winston-Salem, North Carolina, because the town had such close ties to big tobacco. But Great Spirit has a funny sense of humor – of course that's where my Beloved lived, so I had to give up that prejudice in order to be with him. Now I am grateful for Winston-Salem. Its Moravian influence of powerful, self-directed, and generous women has magnetically called many women of high ideals who are interested in creating an equitable and respectful environment for all and are willing to engage with one another to manifest beauty, artistic expression, healing and balance in this region.

When you offer the tobacco bundle with your request, a respectful preface is that you ask that your request be considered. It is seen as ill-mannered to ask point blank, putting the Medicine Healer on the spot to answer right away. When you say, "Would you consider doing a Soul Retrieval Ceremony (or whatever ceremony you have in mind) for me," the Medicine Healer can then always answer yes, they will consider it. That consideration often takes 4 days – one day for each of the four cardinal directions

– to gain clarity from the teachings held in each direction until the big picture is fully understood. The Medicine Healer sits with your request, talking with their Medicine Allies and yours to see if this is the right ceremony, at the right time, and with the right Medicine Healer. When you initiate contact after the 4 days, the Medicine Healer will give you a clear answer whether to proceed, wait until a future time, or go in an altogether different direction.

Yes, sometimes requests are made straight from our heart to Great Spirit – not utilizing tobacco or any other outer protocol. One year I had made this type of request of Rockingbear at a teaching circle he was giving in Chapel Hill. I had identified an inner heart's desire or longing for more ceremony in my life and, in the spur of the moment, made that request out loud to him in front of the audience during the question and answer part of the evening. He just smiled and resumed his teaching on the topic at hand. I knew that if I wanted a specific response from him, I would need to make that request with tobacco. As it turns out, that didn't happen because, almost immediately, people started showing up in my life, asking me to do ceremony for them. When I looked back on that year I realized that I had wanted Rockingbear to do ceremony for me but Great Spirit had other plans – for me to do ceremony for others. My life was now filled with ceremony – my heart's desire had been heard, manifesting in a way that was wholly unexpected. We call that "following the snake." Our path never turns out to be a straight line (even though we have beliefs that it's *supposed* to be that way), but rather like the river or snake, turning this way and that, taking us on a journey that supersedes the shortest route so that we can experience what we need to experience along the way. This is why we don't need to figure out the "how" of our request. All that's needed is simply stating it and the willingness to follow the snake wherever it takes us. Sure makes the journey more fun and, ultimately, a soul-enriching and enlightening involvement with Life. It's what makes us alive! This willingness to follow the signs, omens, portents, and messages that come our way through inner and outer experiences is magical and mystical, feeding the soul and feeding the world – the entire Planetary Family.

Remember that ceremony begins when your request is made and accepted. It may or may not turn out the way you have envisioned or in accordance with your expectations. I have seen with my own requests, and in considering the requests of others, that timing plays a crucial role. Sometimes all the allies and helpers are on board but it is not to be done at this time – that simply means that other work needs to come first, other healing engaged in, often so that the request can be fully fulfilled. When the request is taken to Great Spirit and considered with insights from the Directional Powers, then a true response that fits with your soul's journey is discerned. In this way we are following the snake, attuned to our heart's desires, and working with Divine Timing.

CHOOSING TO BE READY

To fully participate in the Calling Ceremony, you will soon realize that it can't be done by figuring it out with your left brain or controlling all the points and events involved in bringing you together with your Soul Companion. These can only be accomplished through the cosmic connection you have with Great Spirit and with every other being in the Universe. If you think you can do this ceremony alone, think again. It's going to involve all of you – your vast spiritual wisdom and the help of your Spirit Helpers/Guides/Guardian Angels, Animal Totems, Medicine Ancestors and all the other beings in the Universe who are willing to help you. It could be a fellow two-legged, any of the creature beings, a standing person (tree), a stone being, a medicine plant person, or any and all of Creation. Remember how the mountains came to me in the dreamtime journeys, inviting me to the Blue Ridge Mountains? They were assisting me by showing me where I needed to move in order to fulfill the request my heart had made – a native teacher residing on the physical plane – and also to move me closer to my Soul Companion. If I had not listened or heeded the mountain beings, Great Spirit would have found some other voice to get my attention but it may have taken longer or made my journey more troublesome. One woman I know talks about how her Spirit Guides usually have to hit her upside the head with a stick to get her attention! It's funny and your guides are definitely willing to use whatever methods work for you, but the drama of it takes energy and time away from what you are here to do. You can choose to surrender your stubbornness so that you may proceed with grace and ease, clarity and trust. It is up to you to listen and be alert, especially if you actually want your request fulfilled in this lifetime! Or you can wait until you're 80 to begin the life you want to live. It's your choice. You can choose to be ready. You can choose to start listening to and trusting that small, inner voice, your Orenda, to guide and direct you on your path.

As an act of bravery, stand before the full moon on a clear night and tell her "I'm ready." You don't even have to know what you're ready for, just that you are ready. You are making a choice and communicating that choice to Grandmother Moon and the entire Planetary Family. Hold on to your hat though because your life will shift in ways that you never dreamed possible!

INVOKING THE INVISIBLE FLAME OF MANIFESTATION

Nothing happens in the Universe until a request has been made. When we are still in the Spirit World, we call for a physical body and two people answer that request by making a baby. As a baby, we make vociferous requests for food, sleep, warmth, and nurturing. We don't beat around the bush. We are extremely clear about what we need and want. Remember those loud howls coming out of such a little body? As a young child, we often made our requests through statements, "I'm hungry!" "I'm thirsty" or "I want" and we would point at it. As we became more domesticated, we learned to make our requests through questions, "May I have another cookie?" or "Can I go to the movies tonight since my homework is done?" As adults, we need to remember the single-minded focus and clearness of stating what we want and expressing that desire simply, with few words but completely specific, allowing the desire to spring from our deepest inner longing. Making our requests without explanations, rationalizations, or qualifiers frees up the energy behind it so it can be propelled into the world of matter. Making our requests from that inner, childlike part that cannot conceive of not receiving what we need and want when we need and want it, ensures that it can be easily received by all the forces in the Universe. This isn't about being selfish or self-centered; it's about being clear, precise, and simple. It's not a childish demand, it's a request from our childlike knowingness. It's about being full of faith, trust and acceptance that we deserve to live a life filled with purpose, clarity, harmony and love. It is our right as a Being of Light to co-create with Great Spirit.

Our requests cannot be made in the form of a demand nor can we tell Great Spirit how our request or prayer has to be answered. Neither of these ways is from the Orenda but rather from the ego. I'm reminded of the joke that goes along these lines: a man was adrift on the ocean, praying to God to be saved. A boy came along with a raft and wanted to help, but the man waved him off, saying he was praying that God would save him. Then a fisherman came along with a boat, but again the man wouldn't get in the boat, saying he had faith that God would save him. Then a yacht came by and threw him a life preserver and again, he passed it by, saying he was waiting for God to hear his prayer and save him! When we have a fixed idea of how our request is to be answered, we won't be able to recognize the signs, omens and portents – all those messengers – that are responding to and assisting us in reaching our heart's desire or prayer.

When our prayers or requests are orders – we want such and such to happen (preferably right now!) – or we allow our prejudices and personal likes and dislikes to mandate what we will or won't accept – we are not making a request, we are making a demand. If I had put the limitation on Great Spirit that I was calling a Soul Companion to me BUT he couldn't live in Winston Salem because of its connection to the tobacco industry, or his yearly salary had to be a specific amount, or he could only be a certain age, I would have put serious roadblocks in my request, making it almost impossible for Divine Will to be activated in order for synchronicity and magic to play its vital role. I would have been telling Great Spirit how it was to assist me by setting parameters based on my personal likes and dislikes. That's why it's so important to do the preparation of clearing limiting beliefs and prejudices before sitting with the Fire. This difference between making non-limiting but specific requests versus self-sabotaging, limiting demands is incredibly important to our ability to co-create. This became clear to me while doing the Calling Ceremony with Rockingbear as to why all those years before I had been calling for a Soul Companion on my own without any results. I had too many limiting beliefs and prejudices that entangled the whole enterprise, never allowing it to take flight.

Some of us have incredibly strong and powerful personal wills that can manifest solely on our own energy, without requesting and invoking assistance from Great Spirit or Divine Will. I noticed that when I have done this in the past, there is an essential rightness or alignment that never comes to pass. Almost like an empty shell or husk, it looks good from the outside but there's nothing on the inside that will feed the soul for long term sustainability. We are in a partnership with Great Spirit whether we like it or not. It takes a village to help manifest our requests and by village I'm talking about all the members of the Planetary Family – seen and unseen, tangible and intangible, microscopic and vast.

We are also not asking permission, raising our hand and waiting to be called upon by an authority outside of ourselves. When we defer our will to Great Spirit, we are, in essence, giving away some of our power, our passion, our commitment to our life. It is a belief that someone or something outside of ourselves will fix our life, will take command and make sure we don't make any mistakes. As a Co-Creator we give ourselves permission to live our life to the best, highest and fullest ways we can conceive of each and every moment. And once we do, the bar is raised and then we can conceive of better, higher and fuller, and on and on. This is called personal growth, spiritual evolvement, individuation, or enlightenment. We do have free will for a purpose and that is to be a Co-Creator in our life, to take responsibility for our choices, to continue to evolve, to become our vision, to become the change we wish to see in the world while invoking the higher energies of our Allies and Great Spirit to assist us.

So, in summation: no demands or ultimatums, no begging for permission – just requests and prayers from your heart as a Co-Creator. You are specific without being limiting. You make your request through gratitude that you already have it here in the tangible world. You leave the myriad details of how, when and with whom to the realm of Great Spirit which calls forth synchronicity or meaningful coincidences to come into play. Synchronicity is the intersection of your personal will and Divine Will, beyond your ability to control and configure with the ego mind. It is the confluence of your state of consciousness with your connection to the world (seen and unseen) around you. When you are in the right place, at the right time, with the right people, magical things occur. It's really that simple and fun and amazing and natural.

This is dangerous work though – you could end up being happy! So, gather your courage, search your heart and hunker down in your power. You are about to embark on a journey of co-creation, healing and enlightenment in order to bring yourself into an intimate, authentic relationship with your Soul Companion. Be the bravest you can be.

CREATING AN ALTAR

Most of the inner reflective work you will be doing in the Calling Ceremony will be done on your own. You will periodically touch base with the Medicine Healer assisting you, sharing what you have found in your inner excavations and receiving help in discerning other beliefs and limitations that need to be examined, but most of the heavy lifting will be up to you. To aid you in these endeavors, it's helpful to create an altar in your home or personal space. An altar connects us to the ceremony, providing a focal point for contemplation and renewal.

There are many different kinds and forms of altars, some very specific to certain ceremonies and healings as passed down from teacher to student. Some altars are set up permanently while others are created for a particular circle, intention or ceremony and then taken down upon completion. Your altar will be wholly dependent on what speaks to you personally to best hold the energies of who you are and what's most important to you. No two altars will be the same. Simply put, altars are a face upon which certain energies or medicines are honored to help us remember our connection to the Divine. Sacred objects, medicine pieces, stones, bits of bone, hair, hide, feather, teeth or antler of animal totems, plant or tree pieces, photos, or mementos have all been used on altars, and usually in conjunction with the element of water (a bowl or fountain) or fire (a candle or incense) or both together.

Select a space in your home where you can leave this altar in place, if possible. It could be in the middle of your meditation room, or on a side table or mantel or even on a tray that you slide in and out of a shelf or from under the bed. Create whatever works with your home situation or personal space – taking into account pets, children, and other family members who will be present. If you need to set it up in a multi-use space, make sure it is located so that no one is stepping on it or over it or needing to move it when you aren't there. Use a beautiful cloth to delineate the face and then place your objects intentionally upon it. It can be small or large – size isn't as important as the meaning and connection derived from the chosen items.

The altar I created for this ceremony was simple, small and fit easily on the top of a cabinet in my bedroom. It held a candle which I would light when I was actively working with the altar, a photo of me and my son because my Beloved would be in an emotionally intimate, authentic relationship with my son as well, a silver and crystal dragonfly (one of my main totems) I had brought back from Bali years before, a flamingo feather (I wore the name Rainbow Feather at the time of my calling) and a river stone from the place where I first met Rockingbear. I wanted the man coming into my life to see who I was energetically and what held importance to me. This small altar came with me when I sat with the Fire to honor the connection it had given me during my preparations.

Be creative and pay attention to the energies that want to be included on your altar, sometimes it may surprise you! As you go deeper into the Ceremony, if the items on your altar need to be changed or added to, don't hesitate to do so. It needs to reflect who you are in the present moment. It will be your choice as to whether all or some of the sacred items come with you when you sit with the Fire.

Paying Attention

Rockingbear shared that he had found three keys for a happy, fulfilled life. The first one is to pay attention. The second one is to pay attention. And the third one is – you guessed it – to pay attention! The way I use this teaching is by paying attention to my life in three areas – physical, emotional/mental and spiritual. Paying attention means we are listening, observing, feeling and taking note of our inner knowings. We are willing to show up, be present and remain awake. We become spiritual detectives, discerning the who, what, when, where and why of any given situation. Paying attention means taking responsibility for our well-being. We can't make this beautiful, heart-inspired request for our Soul Companion and then fall asleep, assuming that somehow it will come about while we are sleeping or distracted.

By actively listening to our Orenda – that small, still voice – trusting our intuition, paying attention, and staying awake, we can follow the snake in our life. This snake is the way our path unfolds. It's never in a straight linear fashion, but moves in the way a river winds through its landscape. This is how we co-create with Great Spirit. It can look to others like you are not doing what you should be doing, like you are going off course, because they are on a different river with different twists and turns. It doesn't matter what your journey looks like to others. What makes the journey yours is listening to your inner wisdom and letting that be your guide. It will never steer you wrong. You can trust in it completely. Only you can prove to yourself that you can trust your heart, that inner, small voice, and the messages, signs and omens that come from your Spirit Guides. No one else can prove it to you and you can't prove it to anyone else either. Scientists can prove when you are dreaming by monitoring your brain patterns but they can't prove what you were dreaming about. Nevertheless, your dreams are real to you because they are YOUR dreams. This is the way of life as well. These inner promptings – the knowings, feelings, and perceptions – are real but cannot be proven. Don't even try. It's a waste of time. We only try to convince or explain to another when we are unsure of ourselves, when it's simply a belief. When it's a truth that we know within us, we just accept it for what it is and let others accept it or not, based on their understanding. We become free from needing other people's approval or permission to be true to ourselves.

Paying attention to our physical health and well-being means we are listening to our bodies, allowing our physical body to communicate directly with us. Aches and pains, illness and dis-ease are all messages from our body. These messages are waiting to be picked up – like the blinking light on a phone answering machine. Once we pick up the message and act upon it, the physical pain, illness or dis-ease almost always goes away unless there is a deeper spiritual message and further action or non-action is needed. The messages can be about our physical health and well-being, but they can also be broader messages about how to bring balance and healing to our life in general.

Many years ago, I experienced an intense pain in the middle of my back on my right side. It wouldn't go away and actually started hurting along a horizontal line around the right side of my body. I asked my body for the message pertaining to the pain. Being a practicing spiritual detective, I had already discerned that because the pain was on my right side (the masculine side), it most likely had something to do with masculine energy – either within me or someone else. As I sank deeper into an expanded awareness of my body, I realized that I was feeling guilty – guilty that I didn't have the funds to help my father and brother who were both out of work at the same time. I had recently bought my first house and then traded in my car for a new one so I wasn't able to help them. When I accepted that it was okay and I didn't need to feel guilty about it, I felt much better. The pain was a virus called shingles which often manifests more than once, but because I had discerned my body's true message, the virus hasn't shown up again. This experience led to an agreement with myself: that it's okay for me to help and support others to the best of my ability at any given time – that what I can give of myself in that moment is truly enough.

Our bodies are perfectly willing to endure pain and illness so we can learn what we need to learn as we journey on our spiritual path. The same is true for our mental and spiritual observations and experiences. By paying attention to all these signs, we can receive guidance that tells us when we are on the right track or whether we need to speed up or slow down, or move left or right or up or down in order to be in the right place at the right time to connect with the right people. By paying attention to our inner and outer realities, and then making small adjustments along the way, our path unfolds with grace and ease. This state of heightened awareness is often called synchronicity or being in the flow. Yes, there are challenges and trials, sorrow and hardship, but overall it doesn't need to be a struggle to be who we are or to do what we have come to do. Of course, all of this applies as well to the calling of our Soul Companion – paying attention to how we are being led to follow the snake and migrate through our life so that our paths will intersect in wondrous and magical ways.

MARIA'S ODYSSEY

I was in my 40s, alone after a string of relationships with men that had all ended badly. Since adolescence, I had listened to the well-meaning advice of my parents, grandparents, friends and self-help books advocating that the path to marriage was first, by getting yourself to a place where "you no longer need a man" and, second, "When you stop looking, 'The One' will show up when you least expect it." This was later reinforced by the advice I got from all my friends, colleagues, even my ex-relationships who were, for the most part, either married or in the process of breaking up with me. In my mind, this translated into a belief that there was a LOT wrong with me innately that I had to fix: I wasn't pretty enough, skinny enough, smart enough, sane enough or successful enough. In college, I had begun a fast and furious long haul of investing time and money in "bettering myself" through my choice of career, spiritual pursuits, medication, therapy, clothes, weight loss products and every self-help book on the market. I had latched on to just about anything that could make me "appear" better on the outside than I felt on the inside. All of this left me increasingly broken, defeated and miserable. I was mistakenly thinking I would attract the man of my dreams who would solve all the "awkwardness" of being single and childless in your late 30s and 40s.

In 2002, defeated and seeking another "last ditch effort", I began to explore Native American spirituality, but this time, something was different. I stuck with it for the next eight years, sitting in a weekly circle of women with White Star, which didn't, at first, appear to be "working" either. Afterwards, I realized it was simply about being willing to just sit for a couple of hours once a week and be GRATEFUL for something, anything, even if I was so defeated and miserably alone that the only thing I could think of was my gratitude for how spectacularly Matthew McConaughey had kept his body in shape and visible in the movie "Sahara." A movie that I had sat through alone. The native spirituality circle was about taking responsibility for the people, places, events, opportunities and failures I was creating in my life without blame or self-recriminations. It was about shifting my focus from "damage control," for I was indeed elegantly damaged and continuing to embrace ideas, philosophies, diet programs and men who were reinforcing the damage, to being "grateful" for the experience that I wished to have, even if it hadn't shown up yet. And the circle was about gratitude for the day I would no longer have to sit in movies alone or go home from a hard, stressful day of work to an empty apartment, and gratitude for meals and grocery shopping to share and making it easier to sleep at night.

When I began to consider the calling ceremony, I was completely skeptical and thought to myself "This will never work either, but what the hell do I have to lose?" Back then, I had an inkling, but truly no idea of the delightful slog that I was in for. As is typical, the ceremony begins with the exchange of tobacco, a Native American tradition of gifting your intentions or prayers in the form of ground tobacco leaves to an elder for their assistance. It's a very clear and serious decision and commitment, for once the tobacco has changed hands, there's no going back. It's on. My calling ceremony had started.

The ceremony began with me writing an exhaustive list of what I wanted in a man, what I didn't want and getting crystal clear about who this was that I wanted to bring into my life. After filling a hundred rows in an excel spreadsheet outlining his details,

I was told to synthesize it down to one sentence. My one sentence was "Self-cleaning oven," meaning he took care of his own grime and crap and absolutely had that capability built in. I had enough of my own self-cleaning to do and LOTS of experience cleaning up emotional and financial messes in previous relationships that had left me both financially and emotionally spent. Then, I decided to update my social profile on the online dating sites and put myself out there.

Well, therein was the dilemma – I was bringing Mr. "Self-Cleaning Oven" into my life and my life sucked. I didn't like my life, so how, in God's name, would I ever trust "Mr. Self-Cleaning" when he finally showed up? Why would I trust someone who would fall in love with a complete wreck like me? I had thrown myself fully into a toxic work environment, furiously seeking the highest paying jobs I could find with the skills that I had accumulated, trying desperately to correct my financial situation and appear "successful" to "Mr. Self-Cleaning." This vision that I had was of a man who was everything I wanted but who, at that point in time, the time of the calling ceremony, I did not feel I deserved. So, I kept at it the best I could. I then began to solicit attention from the online dating world, as well as a few dates with "friends of friends." The gift here from the work I had done in the calling ceremony was that I knew immediately whether this was "Mr. Self-Cleaning" and could side step the "Hell no's" and give the "maybe's" a little more time. I no longer had to "settle" for an experience that was in any way less than what was on the list that I'd created and turn each date into a long, drawn out sordid drama when it just wasn't right.

I continued, off and on, experimenting with the practice of being grateful for my life and over time (I'm talking about a long time, because clutching stubbornly to concepts that don't serve me has been handed down through generations of women in my family) I began to make different choices and to "call in" my biggest and wildest dreams.

One big dream was to earn an MBA from a reputable school and I found one in Europe that I could afford while working. I began to loosen the strict rules I had believed in for "feeling attractive." It began less and less to be about my family's or culture's view of what "attractive" was and more and more about how I really could begin stepping into self-acceptance, satisfaction and joy through "calling in" what fit me on a soul level. I liked what that kind of "attractiveness" felt like and who it began resonating with. Learning to understand what soul recognition feels like released the previous notions of what "attractiveness" should visually "look like." What resonated with me was allowing myself to be successful in my MBA program – a goal that always seemed appropriate for the men in my career and work life who had been promoted over me, who talked over me in meetings or simply never "saw" me or noticed that I had a valuable contribution to make. What was important for me to learn was that I could emerge from self-defeating choices and actions and stand firm in the wisdom I had gained over the years, in spite of feeling despicable, fat, short, stupid or mentally ill. I was calling a new and different experience. There was indeed a spark of brilliance, love, compassion, wisdom and leadership in me that is sourced from the same spark that is in ALL, but I find is uniquely expressed through each of us individually. This is the spark that I began to feed when I felt it show up, and I learned to make choices that served me. This big dream began to come true and suddenly "Mr. Self - Cleaning" showed up. I fought it initially, but gave in to the realization that both of us had finally shown up for each other years after the Calling Ceremony. There were some bumps in the road but we continued to figure out how to live in joy and contentment together and eventually married.

The calling ceremony is still going on. I continue to "call in" the experiences I wish to have with myself, with him and his children from a previous marriage, with everything in my life, with GRATITUDE. Both the joy and the contentment have increased incrementally over the past thirteen years and I'm no longer alone or in fear all the time. I am responsible for creating the experiences I wish to have in my life and make different choices if the ones I'm making now aren't resulting in what I wish to experience.

I've also learned that needs are legitimate and that I must be very clear about what my needs are in order to "call them in." I also must be very clear about what his needs are in order to support him in their fulfillment but I am totally responsible for my own happiness as he is responsible for his. We just help each other out from time to time. It's very nice now to have help with it, to discover these things about each other joyfully and willingly help each other out, together.

In spite of what the self-help books and my well-meaning friends said, I really do need a man, but not for what I previously thought. It's been fun learning that "the ONE" is learning, through being in relationship, how ONE we really all are and how it's actually up to each of us to make the choices that create the lives we wish to have through conscious gratitude, expressing our thoughts, words and feelings in our own unique, individual way. Over time, I've realized that ceremony is empty unless we can bring ourselves to it. Presence is required. This ceremony, and the entire process involved, was meaningful, and a powerful healing.

North Direction

CONNECTING WITH THE
WISDOM OF THE AGES

○————————————○

"All you SpiritKeepers of the North, Come, Look this way!
We give gratitude for all the ceremonies and teachings that
sustain us, for all you white-haired ones –
you Elders – who carry wisdom for the People.

Thank you, white-furred ones – fox, hare, polar bear –
who live in the place of cold, hard truth,
teaching us to embrace and be grateful for the truth.

Thank you, Buffalo People, for your
medicine of abundance and gratitude.

Thank you, Tall Standing Ones, for your teachings
of longevity, endurance and how to stand
in our power without breaking.

We are grateful to you, Winds of Change,
empowering us to resist complacency."
Wah Doh

PURIFICATION AND TRANSFORMATION

There are many ceremonies for purification and healing to help you ready yourself for the transitions and transformations that will come about through the Calling Ceremony. These healing ceremonies make it easier for you to ride the tsunami of emotions that arise with change. You can help make these transitions an exhilarating, wild, hold-on-to-your-seat kind of ride or you can be overwhelmed and tumbled and dashed onto the sand (gently, or not so gently). Rockingbear called this work "lightening your canoe" because you can only get to where you are going when your canoe is light enough to travel on such a far-reaching and deeply important soul journey. You can lighten your canoe by releasing the thoughts, words, habits, prejudices, judgments, beliefs, and limiting agreements that are no longer serving you. Being as light as possible means you can traverse the rapids, portage easily when you need to, and enjoy the journey – it doesn't have to be so hard. If you find that your life has become a struggle, lighten your canoe. Effort and full engagement is still required but without the undue hardship and unending struggle.

After the first wave of settlers moved westward in a myriad of wagon trains, stories came back to the new settlers who were preparing for their own journeys telling them to not take anything beyond their clothes and small family heirlooms because whatever they needed later could be found by the side of the trail, abandoned by previous settlers when their wagons were too heavy to make it through the tough spots. Our inner journeys are not so different. We have to jettison the heaviness of all the inner clutter we have been lugging around. Some of the baggage isn't even ours! We agreed (usually unconsciously but not always) to carry it for our ancestors, our families, our loved ones and even sometimes for our enemies or nemeses. We can't sustain that weight for long. It takes its toll by showing up as physical illness, dis-ease, depression, and other emotional and spiritual wounds. These burdens often keep us from manifesting our dreams because we are so overwhelmed by the weight of them that we can't move forward – we're stuck. And we all know what being stuck feels like. I love the adage – "Let go or be dragged!"

This is a continual practice for me, excavating my inner landscape to see what no longer fits and what beliefs and other limiting thoughts and habits need to be replaced. Sometimes I initiate the digging, wanting to find what I once buried because at the time I didn't have the inner strength or knowledge to look at it or deal with it, but now I do. And sometimes a hole just appears in front of me on my path, inviting me (usually through a coyote trick on myself) to go down the rabbit hole to better see a part of my belief system more clearly. Either way it is always an opportunity to heal, to shift, to shed, to become more fully the truest expression of my soul.

Below are descriptions of several ancient medicine ceremonies for you to consider that will help you release the burdens and heal the wounds of your life. These ceremonies are found in some form in every indigenous culture. They have been passed down from one generation to the next from Medicine Healer to apprentice in the oral tradition. This way of teaching is most effective for retaining an undiluted, spirit-filled and spirit-filling healing. Being taught from books or the written word is, in many ways, less precise and prone to misinterpretations. Imagine never seeing anyone tie a pair of shoes, only being able to read about how to do it. It would take a long time to figure it out by written instructions, even with illustrations! By seeing it done again and again, and practicing it on our own many times, it becomes effortless and automatic.

This is the way Rockingbear taught me – through teachings, stories and examining my personal experience with the teachings. When I am doing the Soul Retrieval ceremony, I remember my teacher showing me step by step, and that's the same way I do it today. I was taught by my teacher, who was taught by his, and on up the line. Little has changed. A few software upgrades for this time and place but the essence or core of it remains pure after thousands, probably hundreds of thousands of years. Consistency and fully understanding the energetics being worked with have given these ceremonies the power to heal and bring back into balance that which has become confused and damaged within us.

A word of caution: please be aware that not everyone offering ceremony has been trained fully in the intricacies and spiritual knowledge of these ancient ceremonies. When you find someone offering these ceremonies, be a good detective. Find out: Who is their teacher? Did they train for seven years with a Medicine Healer as is traditional or did they take a weekend workshop? How long have they been doing this work? How does their life grow corn? In other words, is their own life a reflection of harmony, balance, abundance, peace, creativity and healing? If they cannot manifest it for themselves, what makes you think they can help you do so. I am happy when people ask me questions before requesting my assistance with ceremony. People often take more care in choosing a hairdresser or a lawn service than choosing the right person to do ceremony with them. From my experience, a Medicine Healer who can do these ceremonies in an impeccable way has taken the time and effort to study with a traditional teacher and healer or with someone who was directly trained by a traditional teacher and healer. There is so much more to a ceremony that the outward appearance or form of it – monkey see does not equate with monkey do.

SOUL RETRIEVAL CEREMONY

Before you are ready to call your Soul Companion to you, you may want to make sure that all of you is there to do the calling. You want to be as whole, complete, balanced, healed and full of self-understanding as you can be before you undertake to bring yourself into intimate relationship with another. One very good, selfish reason is that the more healed you are, the more healed your Soul Companion will be. Remember – like attracts like on the energetic, spirit level. Also, if you aren't whole and complete, you may look to your Soul Companion to fill those voids within you and, of course, that is ultimately not possible, even if in the short run it appears to be. If we are a puzzle with pieces missing, we may think that others hold our missing pieces, when, in reality, they are probably missing some too and are hoping we have theirs! But we cannot fill those inner voids for each other. Recently I saw this quote: "One day, someone is going to hug you so tight that all of your broken pieces will stick back together." It's a lovely thought; however, I haven't found this to be true. Could it really be true that if a loved one doesn't hug us tight enough or love us deeply enough we won't heal the addictions that control us, or the emotional wounds that sap our strength, or the illness that can manifest from soul loss? No. When we have pieces missing, those pieces have broken off due to trauma, accident or illness and are now in other worlds, no longer accessible to us. A Medicine Healer is trained to travel to other worlds, track down any missing pieces of the soul, retrieve your pieces (and not some other person's pieces that are similar!) and bring them back to you.

The Soul Retrieval Ceremony is one of the ancient, powerful ceremonies handed down from generation to generation and found in every indigenous culture for healing – bringing back into wholeness that which has been splintered. In this ceremony, pieces of the soul that broke off due to trauma – physical, emotional, or spiritual – or pieces that were taken without permission are found in the Spirit World and returned to you so that you are once again a complete, whole being. People who have experienced soul loss share some the following symptoms: a feeling that something is missing inside, continually searching for something their whole life but not really knowing what they are searching for, a feeling that there is something for them to do this lifetime but they can't quite grasp what it is, or they have an inkling of their purpose or mission but don't know how to accomplish it. Sometimes there are pervasive, unexplainable feelings of sadness, hopelessness, grief or anger that never completely go away no matter how good their life is at the moment. Many people are aware that they are missing parts of themselves, but they aren't aware that there is a ceremony to bring those pieces back.

Experiencing soul loss is somewhat like a committee coming together to plan and put on a big event, but the people who have the most knowledge and experience aren't able to show up. The rest of the committee can muddle through, doing the best they can, but it's a lot harder for them than it needs to be and some parts just won't get done. Think how much easier and fuller the final event would be if the people who have the expertise show up and participate in the planning and execution. It's the same in your life. When all of you is there to do what you've come to do, it's a lot easier. It can even be fun and fulfilling!

During the Soul Retrieval Ceremony, the more *nothing* you do, the better! The Medicine Healer goes into the Invisible World or Spirit World to see if you have pieces missing. You won't know for sure if you have pieces missing until the Shaman goes and looks.

It's rather like going to the dentist to check for cavities. If your tooth hurts, you may surmise there is a cavity but until the probing and x-rays are completed, you don't know for sure how many and on which teeth. Similarly, in this ceremony, you may have a sense that something is missing inside yourself or that you are not all present and accounted for. The Shaman journeys to see if you have any pieces missing, how many and at what age they left. According to my training, I don't journey to look until we are in the ceremony and ready to retrieve those pieces. Sometimes the pieces have been taken without your consent, and then we have to move purposefully into the World of the Dead to retrieve them. The less notice of intent the better. It's rather like rescuing hostages. The less notice of activity, the better and easier it is to retrieve those pieces of the soul. Your responsibility during the ceremony is to open yourself up as much as possible and create a space for the missing pieces to return home. It's hard to welcome home parts of your soul if you are full of mental machinations, limiting thoughts and a closed heart. Who wants to return home to find there is no space for them?

After the pieces are returned and blown back into you, you begin dialoging with each piece so you can learn what it wants you to do in your life for it to stay with you. These pieces often leave due to trauma and violence – either a physical accident, an illness or emotional trauma involving fear, hurt, guilt, and pain. Or a piece of your soul can be taken if you were spiritually unprotected and vulnerable to a theft, usually at a young age. I have found that many times a piece has been taken by a loved one who thought they needed your energy or part of you in order to survive or because they felt entitled to it because of their love for you. But this kind of action must be called something other than love. It is about entitlement, ignorance and fear of not having what they need. Many times when a piece of the soul has been taken without consent, the taker has a piece of their own soul missing and is trying to fill that hole the only way they know how. Sometimes you can unwittingly give a piece of yourself away, thinking that this form of self-sacrifice will heal someone else or that it proves how much you love someone. But this is not the case. You only hurt yourself and, ultimately, you also hurt the one to whom you have given a piece of yourself. I share these scenarios so that you can more fully check within yourself to see if the Soul Retrieval Ceremony is needed as you enter into the Calling Ceremony.

The Soul Retrieval Ceremony is life changing, incredibly healing and priceless. To be whole once again is truly the greatest gift you can give yourself. But this Ceremony isn't a magic pill, making everything in your life instantly okay. Eventually, though, when all of your soul is present to solve problems, chart your course and take the necessary actions, life becomes an exciting journey rather than an insurmountable struggle. After the ceremony, your ongoing work is to keep your word with the pieces that have come back. During the ceremony, those pieces have shared with you about what they need you to do in your life now and you state whether you are willing to make those changes. Often it is a commitment on your part to be true to yourself, to live with love and joy and to drop the limitations of fear, guilt and suffering that were learned to cope with the soul loss. These pieces have not been embodied for quite a while, sometimes from the time you were in utero! So they are more purely spirit, just like a newborn or toddler. These parts of yourself have incredible amounts of energy, clarity, wisdom and spiritual understanding of who you are, what you are here to do and how to do it. They will be essential in calling your Soul Companion into your life. Their wisdom and knowledge will add so much to your intentions and you may feel, after the ceremony, that you are calling someone entirely different into your life than you would have called before the Soul Retrieval. In essence, you will be a new person because you are whole and complete! Your old language, the way you think and talk about yourself, changes because you have other options, viewpoints and abilities available to you now. This cannot help but create a different frequency for your calling. As a whole, complete being, you will call another whole, complete being into your life so that you can each be the person the other has been asking for.

Once those pieces of your soul are reunited with you, you will find that you are standing in such a powerful place; one that you haven't stood in for a very long time. So there is an integration component. If your pieces integrate quickly, you will feel the changes and power immediately. Sometimes it takes a bit longer to integrate – the changes in thoughts, feelings, and ways of being may happen over several days, weeks and even, occasionally, months. One man shared that it was 6 months after his ceremony when he realized he was in a completely different place in his life, free of the angst and feelings of separateness that he had lived with for so long. Occasionally, if a person doesn't keep their word in the agreements made, falling back into old habit and thought patterns – the coping mechanisms that were employed to fill the void of the missing pieces – the returned pieces of their soul may leave again, unable to stay. Usually these are people that are working all by themselves without a teacher or mentor. Often they are surrounded by family and friends who don't want them to change because that would mean the family and friends have to change as well. Surround yourself with people who are willing to support you, people you trust with your life, people who have integrity in their lives, who will mirror the truth back to you as you begin living your life as a whole, complete being.

CUTTING CEREMONY

Another valuable and life-changing ceremony is the Cutting Ceremony. It is used to cut away the energetic cords that bind you to the habits, thoughts, fears, and beliefs that no longer serve you on your journey and then to fill that void with positive, joyful energy of your choosing. You can begin by asking yourself how much of your energy, strength and mental clarity is being drained by the past and the hold it has over you? You can make a conscious choice to no longer have negative or destructive habits, thoughts or people in your life. Once you realize that you don't want to drag those heavy burdens around, tripping you up and making you too weary to think clearly, you are ready for the cutting ceremony. You have to let go of the past when you are calling someone new into your life because you are essentially calling a whole new life to yourself. Once you are with your Soul Companion, your life will never be the same. And that's what you want!

One type of Cutting Ceremony has to do with releasing or giving away shame, guilt, fear, and powerlessness experienced in past relationships, and cutting the cord to past lovers. Whenever we have sexual or intimate relationships with another, we are open to an attachment or energy cord being made between us. This attachment can continue on after the actual physical relationship is over. This cord holds the hopes, the unfulfilled promises and the dreams that we carried in our hearts for these relationships. It doesn't matter if the other person didn't carry the same dreams as we were carrying – this is our creation and attachment. By having an attachment to another, we are either pulling energy from them with our yearning and unresolved feelings, or we are being sucked dry of energy by their yearnings and unresolved feelings for us. By cutting the attachment, we are freeing both of us so we can truly grieve, release the energy that was invested in those dreams and move on. Until that happens, a part of us is still living in the past with all the hurts, pain, suffering, dreams, hopes and desires of something that is no longer physically possible. How can we hope to call in our new life with a Soul Companion with such heavy baggage? We don't want to take on another's past baggage any more than they want to take on ours. This preparation is about becoming as clear, balanced and healed as we can be before we make our Calling.

I'm not talking about cosmetic changes so that we look good on the outside, but deep, intensive, honest work on ourselves so our spiritual foundation is as firm as possible before we add another person to the mix. You owe it to yourself and your Soul Companion to take the time to do this inner clearing. Now is not the time to be in a rush and skip over the hard parts. I was single for 20 years for a reason! It took me that long to do the work I needed to do on myself, to be in the physical, emotional and spiritual space I needed to be in so that I could be ready for a relationship with my Soul Companion. There was many a night and day I railed against Great Spirit for taking so long, but there were many inner obstacles I had to clear before I was prepared for the deep, soul-connected type of relationship I dreamed could be real. My personal obstacles involved a sense of false pride and low self-esteem (these two often go together – ping-ponging back and forth), a fear of being vulnerable, and a level of cynicism that tried to mask my insecurities. Because I started my spiritual training at such a young age, I also felt too different from the average person, being comfortable only in spiritual or ceremonial settings. It's taken quite a while for me to be comfortable in purely social situations, and even now I can only tolerate them in short duration. Only by doing the inner work on these and many other aspects of the fear, guilt and hurt within, and continuing this inner healing work, have I been able to be in an authentic, intimate relationship with my Soul Companion. He did his own version of healing himself to be ready for me. And now we continue that inner work – each in our own way, in the traditions that speak to us.

I'm not suggesting that your inner clearing work will take 20 years, but when you look back to see when you actually started, it'll be longer than you thought. Be as honest, impeccable and pure as you can be about what is holding you in the past and be as brave as you can be to have the inner strength to cut it loose, letting it go with love and gratitude – all those past experiences have helped to make you who you are today.

This type of cutting is usually done in ceremony with a medicine knife or a machete and a fire. If using a machete, find a stick from the yard or woods – of whatever length and girth you are drawn to – and while holding the stick, visualize and feel the energy of the attachment that you have ascertained no longer fits in your life going into the stick. When you feel that all the energy of that attachment has been transferred, set it down on top of two pieces of wood so that the center of the stick is between the two pieces. This way you can easily chop it in two with the machete (make sure the machete has been sharpened – a dull tool isn't much help). Once you have placed your stick upon the pieces of wood, you won't touch it barehanded again. With the machete firmly grasped in your dominant hand and with no one standing behind you, raise the machete and with intention and conviction slice the stick into 2 pieces. If you discern that you need more cutting, you can line up one or both pieces to be cut again, using tongs or 2 other sticks – just not your hands. Once you feel complete, that the attachment has been fully cut, all the pieces of the stick are put into the Fire to be transformed. For me, there is a special significance to using a machete in ceremony. In many parts of the world, great violence has been done with machetes, and in this transformative work the machete can be of service in a good way.

Margaret came to me for a cutting ceremony, desiring to cut the attachment to her addiction to being a doormat for other people to abuse and misuse. She was clear that she was ready to do this energetic work – she had reached a point where she knew her life depended on her letting go of the beliefs handed down to her through her family of origin and reinforced through her friendships and personal relationships. She picked a stick about 2 inches in diameter, which is pretty thick for this ceremony. She was determined though, so we went ahead. She swung the machete time after time, but it kept bouncing off the stick. She gathered herself for a final intentional swing and again it bounced. Margaret was ready to give up, but I knew if she didn't cut that stick, she would resign herself to staying the way she had always been. So I went into the shed and brought out the hatchet. No success. Then out came the ax and Margaret's eyes opened wide. She had never swung an ax before. I was determined that we would persevere no matter how long it took or what tool we needed to use. So Margaret practiced a few times with the ax, getting a feel for the heft and weight. We practiced the yell she would use with the swing – a way for her life force to be engaged, adding power to the physical act she was undertaking. It took a few attempts, but finally she was able to chop that stick into 2 pieces. Inwardly, I heaved a sigh of relief – I didn't need to bring out the chainsaw! Which I would have done if needed because she was going to be successful – no matter what. It was a pleasure to see Margaret radiating with joy and happiness when those 2 pieces were given to the Fire to complete the release. She chose to replace those old beliefs and habits with a sense of her own worth, self-respect and determination to set her boundaries with love and conviction.

If using a knife for the ceremony, a piece of twine or yarn can hold the energy of the attachment. The same holds true of not touching it with bare hands once you are ready to cut and, when complete, putting all pieces into the Fire. There are other materials I have seen used that work just as well – your imagination is the limit! Once a group of women used household extension cords and shears to do the cutting. The act of severing the physical cord into pieces completes the intention of letting it go and then the Fire does its work of transforming the attachment into positive energy that we can utilize in our forward momentum. (Obviously, the extension cords were not put into the Fire – no plastic or metal, please.) While the pieces are burning, it's helpful to journey with the beat of the drum to replace what was just released. The Universe doesn't support a vacuum and so we need to intentionally replace the old belief, fear or habit with the truth – whatever is true for us in that moment that supports our continued growth and evolution.

One time a woman came to Rockingbear for help in releasing the fear she was feeling about going up on the mountain for 4 days and 4 nights in the Vision Quest Ceremony. Rockingbear instructed her to use a rope – to tie one end to a tree in her yard and, while holding onto the other end, to yell at her fear, "Let me go!" She did as he instructed but came back the next week saying the fear was still there. She was told to do it again and to yell louder and longer. The third week she came back all smiles. In the midst of her yelling, she realized she simply needed to let go of her end of the rope! Sounds easy, but when we believe something has a grip on us, it can take a while to realize that we are the ones holding on. Simply letting go is a choice – and it's okay to make that choice again and again and again.

I have cut many of my own cords and attachments over the years – often the same ones or a variation on the theme when it's a big lifetime teacher for me. Each time I feel lighter, with more clarity and personal power. Other attachments I have cut once and never looked back. The ceremonial act of putting these give-aways into the Fire for transformation, transmutation and release is important work. Disentangling ourselves from the personal and collective past frees that energy for the future we are creating. Rockingbear graphically stated, "This work of cutting cords is akin to burying the dead bodies you have left stinking in the sun, smelling up your life and polluting your thoughts and actions." He definitely had a way with words! It's a strong image but it sums up very well how we sabotage and pollute our lives with these toxic cords and attachments to the past, to the beliefs that were handed to us without examination from our family of origin and society, and to the habits and addictions that keep us in bondage.

The second type of Cutting Ceremony deals with a situation that involves another being – either in a physical body or not, either in the present or a past lifetime – who has an energy cord attached to you for the sole purpose of taking energy. Sometimes these types of people are referred to as spiritual vampires. If this is the case or you suspect it might be, a Medicine Healer can go into the energetic, intangible world and cut the cord between you. Then your energy can once again build and flow freely within your chakra or energy system. It also allows for the possibility that the other person who was taking energy from you can now choose to feed their soul in a different way – directly from Source or Great Spirit, which is every soul's birthright. When this basic truth of our connection to Great Spirit and the ever-flowing fount of pure energy that is available to each of us is forgotten, then the impulse to take energy from another may seem valid. But it is a temporary lifeline at best and, at worse, sucks or drains the life force from another. It's similar to a drowning person pulling their rescuer under and both drowning. It's never ok for someone to feed off our energy – even when we love them. It's always ok to become a hollow bone to allow universal healing energy and light to come through us to be transmitted and sent to another – we aren't talking about that. A spiritual vampire takes energy whenever they want and in whatever quantity they want with no regard for our personal well-being. With the help of the Medicine Healer, this type of parasitic relationship can be cut, allowing your own energy stores to achieve equilibrium once again and assisting the other being in remembering how to connect directly to Source for energy. It can become apparent after this type of healing that there are some people that we cannot be around and still respect and honor ourselves. With understanding, we can learn to set boundaries for our physical and spiritual wholeness, standing in our power to say no when to not do so depletes and endangers our health and ability to manifest our life with grace and ease.

If you suspect that you are the one acting like a spiritual vampire through a misguided sense of entitlement, possessive love, or desiring power over another, please start working with a Medicine Healer to help you cut your attachment or habit to working with energy in this way. You are harming yourself and the person from whom you are taking energy. This harmful way of being in relationship with yourself and others can be healed. All it takes is the sincere desire to change, grow and evolve. Remember: you are pure energy that cannot be created or destroyed, you are vast and infinite, and connected to Great Spirit at all times. There is no lack or scarcity of energy because everything in the Universe is energy which still doesn't give you the right to take energy from others. You always have all the energy you need to heal and thrive when you keep your connection to Divine Source open and strong. The soul naturally moves towards healing, if you listen to your heart and make choices from that wisdom.

TWIN HEART DREAMING CEREMONY

The Twin Heart Dreaming is a ceremony that was shown to me by the 13 Original Clan Mothers to help those who wish to heal their hearts of old pain, hurts, fears of intimacy, emotional numbness, and/or grief. These unhealed wounds can fester, releasing pain and toxins into our bodies and lives, crippling our desire and ability for intimate, authentic relationships – not only with others but also with ourselves. Sometimes the energy of the heart isn't even really there – perhaps given away through fear of losing someone or a longing for union, or stolen in moments of betrayal and revenge. If this is the case, then when you are ready to reclaim your heart, it is retrieved and brought back to you, ready for further healing if need be.

When I was first offering the Clan Mother Circle in Houston, Texas, a woman from the circle came to me in great distress. Through the teachings of the Clan Mothers, Marie had become aware that there was a heavy, empty space where her energetic heart should be. She felt that this lack of heart was connected with an ex-lover who had treated her badly. She asked if I would help her to heal. Now, this was before I met Rockingbear and entered into an apprenticeship with him to learn the healing ways and ceremonies. So, I took her request to the Clan Mothers in the Turtle Council House in the Spirit world where they do their healing work. I asked the Clan Mothers how we should best proceed and they showed me this ceremony to heal the emotional wounds sustained in dysfunctional relationships. Marie was my guinea pig as I followed the instructions set out by the Clan Mothers. What I found was a connection between Marie and this ex-lover that extended to a previous lifetime where he had been her teacher and mentor who turned on her, betraying her trust and cutting out her heart in a quest for more power. I was sent into the Underworld to retrieve her heart and was taken to the Lake of Hearts. With assistance from my Animal Totems and the Clan Mothers, we were able to locate hers and return it to her, first taking out the stone that had been put in its place energetically all those years before. It was an amazing experience for me and for Marie as I saw in action the healing power of shamanic ways.

This Ceremony works with the Heart Chakra – the connector between the physical and spiritual planes, the conscious and unconscious, and the three lower and three higher chakras. The Heart Chakra holds the true essence of who we are, without any social programming or fears and limitations. Opening and healing whatever has blocked this Chakra gives your life and relationships a depth and intensity of joy that is a source of personal power and healing abilities. It is possible for us all to be healed healers.

During the Ceremony, the healing powers of the 13 Original Clan Mothers in the Turtle Council House (now in the Spirit World) are invoked through shamanic drumming to assist in your healing request. This is an opportunity to experience a deep and powerful healing to reclaim your heart – healed, whole and filled with light, joy and the courage to give and receive true love in your life. This ceremony releases and replaces what no longer serves you, embracing a level of trust and compassion for the journey taken thus far, and the strength of will and open-heartedness to continue the journey of being the highest expression of your true self.

When I was in circle with Rockingbear and at his teaching circles, he would drum for us to journey into the Dreamtime to receive messages, healing, and renewal of our sense of being at-one-ment with the entire Planetary Family. He would always share, "My elders tell me that each and every time we dream with the drum, we can completely heal our lives." I love this teaching and have experienced healing time and time again for myself through the years when dreaming with the drum. I've seen the healing benefits for others who dream with the Clan Mothers in the Turtle Council House. It's the most natural thing we can do – engaging our imagination (the name we call the portal between the intangible and tangible worlds) and allowing our inner eyes to see, our inner ears to hear, and our senses and perceptions to feel and know. We all did this naturally as children, and with opportunity and intention we can recover this ability to go deep within and connect with Great Spirit for answers, healing, transformation and comfort.

If you don't have access to a Medicine Healer to drum for you, you can journey to a drumming CD or drum for yourself and dream at the same time. I recorded a drumming CD, *Medicine Ancestors*, so that people could journey more easily when they don't have a drummer available. The Medicine Ancestors love to hear the drum – it's such a part of our evolution as a species. Sometimes when we are drumming together in the Clan Mother Circle we hear a high-pitched chanting coming from the Grandmothers. It always gladdens my heart and brings tears to my eyes that we are being joined by the Old Ones. When our hearts are open, all things are possible – wondrous, magical, unexplainable, natural. This is what healing is all about.

VISION QUEST CEREMONY

There are many forms of the Vision Quest Ceremony found in all the indigenous traditions. For some it may entail a walk-about – from the aboriginal people of Australia – or a journey by oneself to find an animal totem or other familiar to work with. For others, it could be sitting on a mountain site for 4 days and 4 nights without food or water to cry for a vision, or sitting each month in silence during the 3 heaviest flow days of a woman's Moontime, or dancing for 4 days and 4 nights in a Sacred Dance Arbor. The intention for all of these forms is to set aside our fears, social conditioning, and accepted limitations in order to embrace a level of freedom and expansion found only by directly communing with Great Spirit.

I have had the privilege and honor to participate in many Vision Quest Ceremonies as offered through Rockingbear's personal vision – a dozen times in the support camp for questers on the mountain and also twice being the questor sitting on the mountain. To quest, you take whatever you need to be warm and dry for 4 days and 4 nights. Through ritual preparations for purification and cleansing done months ahead of time and then again the night before and the morning of the first day, a shedding occurs of the social self – the domesticated part of ourselves – until the true self emerges. A lightening of our canoe is the intention so we can travel further more easily and actually enter the realm of clarity and discernment for a vision to come upon us. We take no food or water. We leave the support of our physical bodies to the ones in the support camp. Even though we can't see or hear each other, the supporters eat and drink for those who are questing so they can give their full attention to receiving a vision. Because we are all interconnected, we can support each other this way. In the support camp, a ceremonial Fire is maintained for the 4 days and 4 nights, with the Vision Quest Chief and Fire Chief energetically checking on the questers to see how best to support them on their Vision Quest. It is an intense, complex and totally exhilarating experience to walk up the mountain with human fears, concerns, doubts and ego and four days later walk back down the mountain with peace, trust, clarity and attunement. Even those supporting in the base camp are involved in their own vision quest – just in a different way.

In *The Thirteen Original Clan Mothers*, Jamie shares a traditional feminine way of questing each month for a year. You remove yourself from your ordinary life to commune with that month's Clan Mother to receive dreams, insights and messages from her teachings and her totems and familiars. It's usually the 2-3 days of the heaviest blood flow of your moon cycle but can be any 2-3 days that work best for you. It could be the 2-3 days around the Full Moon or the New Moon, especially if you no longer have a moon cycle for whatever reason. Water and simple fare is available – either prepared ahead by you or provided by a close friend and left each day without encroaching on your time of inward reflection. Your monthly quest could be with a small fire that you keep going at night, or at a retreat center or ashram where they bring food to you, in your own home, or outdoors in a tent – whichever way works for you and your lifestyle. The possibilities are limitless – there is no wrong way to do it. The main ingredient is that you have removed yourself from ordinary life – no phones or internet, reading or craft projects, household duties or family and/or work obligations – simply dreaming, resting, communing, musing, and replenishing. Some women have journaled and/or made drawings to record the thoughts, feelings and images that emerge. At the end of that year, your quest culminates with a 3 - 4 day retreat where close women friends bring you a jug of water and traditional blue corn cakes or other simple fare once a day, leaving them outside your door or the circle of prayer ties defining your personal boundaries, to sustain you but not interfere with you. This is a gentle and wholly effective way of seeking a vision and communing with the Clan Mothers and Great Spirit for insight, healing and spiritual growth.

For several years I offered a Healing Quest for women who made an annual commitment to come together in ceremony for one weekend each month. This was a time for replenishment and recharging, for creation and manifestation work with our hands, and for sitting with the Fire while sharing stories, receiving teachings and doing ritual and ceremony together with the Clan Mothers. By taking time for yourself in this way, you get to know yourself more deeply, clearing out the dead debris, and planting new seeds in your life. It is an extraordinary gift to give to yourself – to be with other like-minded women where it is safe and secure to explore the unexplored within yourself. The love, compassion, excitement and awe engendered with this level of exploration is, of course, contagious! Others see you in a new light and welcome new ways to be in relationship with you. And as you become healed and whole, it ripples out to your family, friends and loved ones, helping others to awaken and heal for themselves.

Whichever way you choose to experience a Vision Quest, it is an undertaking well worth the time and energy involved. It can literally save your life – giving you a renewed sense of self, of where you want to go in your life and with whom you want to walk with on your journey.

Praying with the Sacred Pipe

There are many forms of Pipe Ceremony and each is a beautiful and sacred way to honor our connection to Great Spirit. Sitting in Pipe Ceremony is spiritually replenishing as we share our prayers and gratitudes to Creator. When I first heard personal prayers said out loud, I was in a Sweat Lodge Ceremony outside of Houston, Texas. It brought tears to my eyes to hear the beautiful, heartfelt words spoken with such reverence and honor – especially when the men prayed (it was a mixed sweat). I wasn't able to say my prayers out loud at that time – I was too shy and self-consciousness. But I have since opened and activated my voice – to speak my truth in the best way I know how, to voice my prayers and gratitudes – knowing that when I direct the air from my lungs to flow over my vocal cords to create sound, it is the purest gift I can give. It's a powerful thing – the spoken word. I even sing my prayers now which was a whole other relinquishment of fear for me.

Sitting in circle with others, hearing their prayers, offering your own, receiving the Pipe, smoking it if you wish and otherwise simply holding it in your arms as you would a babe, is hypnotic, relaxing, rejuvenating and joyful. Rockingbear taught that it's more important to bear witness to the prayers of others than to be formulating our own prayers. In this way, we stay present. When we receive the pipe and it's our turn to pray, we speak from the heart, not from words rehearsed ahead of time.

In November of 2000, I was participating in a Pipe Ceremony in Asheville to pray in support of the Vision Questors in Mexico who were going up on the mountain the next morning. There were two pipes present and each was being sent around the circle. When it was my turn to pray with the first pipe, I shared my prayers for the questors and my gratitudes, especially ones pertaining to my Soul Companion. I gave thanks for his life and for all the good work I had done to be ready for him and, likewise, all the good work he had done in his life to be ready for me. I completed my prayers and passed the pipe to the next person. A little while later, the second pipe came to me and again I spoke from my heart about the Soul Companion that I had called to be in my life (remember, I hadn't met him yet in the physical). Then with no conscious thought or forewarning, I blurted out, "And, Great Spirit, I wish he would hurry up!" Well, everyone laughed, as did I – ceremony is real life, not meant to always be serious. The next weekend was Thanksgiving. I visited relatives in Virginia and when I returned home, I found an email waiting for me on the online dating service where I was registered. The email was from a man who turned out to be my Soul Companion and it was the start of our correspondence which eventually led to our meeting in the physical – that's how powerful the Pipe Ceremony is. Our prayers are lifted up by the smoke of the medicine plant in the Pipe and transmitted directly to Great Spirit.

The other magical part of the story of how we met is this: On Thanksgiving Day, my Beloved decided to look at the online dating service where he was registered, which he hadn't visited for quite some time. He used the parameters of the area codes closest to Winston Salem to pull up potential profiles. He entered 336, 704 and 919 (the area codes closest to him), and my profile popped up with my picture. He is highly visual and has a photographic memory for faces so when he saw my picture, he recognized me but couldn't place where we had met. Then my profile blipped off the screen and he couldn't retrieve it. He remembered reading, in the instant my profile was up, that I lived in Asheville which didn't fit the area code parameters he had put in. He looked up Asheville's area code, entered 828, and my profile came back up on the screen. Finally, it came to him that he had seen me in a past life regression where we both lived in a small village in the jungle. He wrote me a one-line email, "please look at my profile and if interested, we can talk together," which I received when I returned from visiting family. He found me with just a wee bit of help from the computer gods and goddesses and my prayers!

GRATITUDE – THE POWER THAT FUELS YOUR CALLING

All births begin with conception. Our requests are no different. We are an active part of the conception. It cannot take place without us. **The true desire held in our heart of hearts is the life force that impregnates the Cosmos where all possibilities reside.** Once the dream request has been conceived, our work is to pay attention so we are in the right place at the right time with the right people for the birth to happen naturally, easily and joyfully. We nurture our unborn dreams through gratitude. By expressing gratitude for our lives, our blessings, and all that we are calling into our lives as though it is already there, we are honoring the gestation, the invisible growth leading to the birth of our dreams. It is not a coincidence that it often takes 9 months or 10 moons for our calling to show up. I did my calling ceremony for my Soul Companion in January and met my partner online in late November so sometimes it takes a little longer! I was more than ready to birth the relationship I was calling into my life. For some, it appears much sooner. It will show up right on time, just in the nick of time, or ahead of what we think is the schedule because Divine Timing is at work in our requests. It is always the perfect time. It takes as long as it takes. We can't push the river as our impatience would like to do. But our fears can slow it down. We have to be long distance runners – sometimes our dream can take many years or more than one lifetime to manifest depending on how many people are involved in our dream and how much healing it entails. Sometimes our dream shows up so quickly we are amazed and say, "Wait, I'm not ready!" The manifestation of a request can happen almost instantaneously. When people come to the Healing Circle with a healing request, honing their request is half of the healing. Just by stating their request, the healing begins. It can be that simple. My son always laughs when he asks me a question about a problem he's been trying to figure out. As soon as the question leaves his lips, the answer comes to him! Or he's looking for but not finding something and when he asks me to help him, he finds it right away. By making the request, we bring it into being. Sometimes it just takes a bit longer for it to show up in the physical.

Don't give up before the miracle happens! Be ready to go the distance with your dreams, to go beyond the timespan of one lifetime if necessary. Black Elk waited and waited for the vision he was given to come about. He died disheartened because it did not manifest in his lifetime. It came later. Many of the Ghost Dancers from the Plains tribes, who were dancing to bring back the old ways and vanquish their enemies (the whites) who were annihilating them and their way of life, were filled with grief and sorrow that they had failed when nothing changed. They were heartbroken and bereft. But in a vision I received in Pipe Ceremony, I saw that because the Ghost Dancers had made the requests and prayers that the old ways return and be honored, and had danced them into Mother Earth for her to hold until the time was right, they set into motion the energy needed to bring back those old ways. Because those prayers were danced then, they are manifesting now. It didn't happen in their lifetime but the old ways are returning, the ceremonies are being honored again and the healing of broken agreements has begun. We need to move beyond the limitation of a preconceived time frame, especially for our collective dreams. What we dream and do today does make a difference for the next seven generations. What we pray for and make requests for now does create a different reality for our children's children and for ourselves when we next incarnate. The Hopi elders tell us "We are the ones we have been waiting for." We will reap the benefit of our requests and prayers for healing, peace and harmony. We are creating our future today with our thoughts, words and actions.

When you accept that you are co-creating your life with Great Spirit, you become more responsible for your life, your choices become powerful, and your actions and non-actions hold creation in the balance. We are not creating our life by ourselves. We are co-creating with every other being on the Web of Life. We are interconnected with All Our Relations on levels of which we are just beginning to catch a glimpse. As spiritual beings we are huge, with tremendous depth, height and breadth. Our logical mind cannot fathom how vast and powerful we truly are. We are so much more than what we experience through the senses of our physical body, worn just for this lifetime. In the Native Traditions, when a person dies, it is said that she has dropped her robe. That is what the physical body is for us – a covering or envelope for our spiritual consciousness. A great example of consciousness informing a physical body is seen in the movie *Avatar* where a human remotely animates a genetically engineered alien body through a hybrid connection of consciousness to the body. In essence, we are all Avatars – our true spiritual selves animating the physical body made for us through procreation!

When we live from a spiritual understanding of who we are and what we have come here to do, our requests are bigger, more encompassing, with greater compassion for life. We know that our requests are interacting with all other requests, constantly re-membering or re-weaving the Web of Life. If the requests are full of greed, power over others, manipulation and control, hatred and violence, then strands of the Web of Life become thin, decayed and broken. It may take a while for the Web to show this decay and the sickness will often show up in other ways, in future generations. Requests that are full of gratitude, joy, love, compassion and respect for all of life restore the Web, healing the strands, creating a strong and resilient weaving to hold the greatness and beauty of Life. This Web of Life feeds us all, and it is our honor to return the love and gratitude that feeds the Medicine Ancestors and all the beings of the Planetary Family that make up the Web of Life.

We each have the opportunity and the right to call into being a life of healing, of wisdom, of respect, of trust, of love, of interconnectedness, of beauty. Rockingbear called this the Beauty Way. We call all this into physical manifestation, one day at a time. Every day. Each day that we awaken and open our eyes is, in essence, a new lifetime. Our life doesn't have to be the way it was yesterday or the day before. We can change and evolve. This is our true nature – co-creating with Divine Will or Great Spirit. Each day with the rising of Grandfather Sun is a new beginning, another opportunity to be the best, highest expression of our Soul.

When we make a request, we state that request in the form of gratitude that we already have what we are requesting. We just haven't seen it yet in the physical world. In the Cherokee way, if we were to pray for rain, for example, the request might sound something like this: "Creator, we give thanks for this abundant pure water that quenches our thirst and waters all these plant beings and tall standing ones in such a good way; we are grateful for the plenty all around us, the green growth and health we see everywhere. Thank you Cloud People for opening yourselves and sharing with us your life-giving rains. Our hearts are full of gratitude to you Water Beings for your purity, your willingness to cycle from earth to sky and back to earth for the benefit of us all." By stating our gratitude for already having it, we are creating an energetic container for what we are requesting to come to us. That container holds the resonating pattern of our request, magnetizing it into physical existence. When we pray and share our requests with Great Spirit in this way, we are holding the truth that we already have it, it just needs to appear in the physical realm so we can use the physical senses of touch, taste, seeing, hearing and smell to perceive it.

My heart is filled with gratitude for all the healing and growth in my life – for each and every person in my life and how they show me all the varied parts of myself. I'm grateful for these ancient teachings that are so applicable and helpful in our so-called modern world. I'm grateful for The Beauty Way and how these indigenous traditions help me stay sane and grounded, awake and aware, positive and willing to continue to co-create a world filled with respect and the peaceful expression of my talents, abilities and skills. I'm grateful for gratitude!

CATHERINE'S DREAM EXPLORATION

What came up for me in this calling ceremony had to do with worthiness. The preparation and the ceremony itself were powerful. I had dreams that informed me in no uncertain terms of what my challenges looked like regarding attracting a mate.

One enigmatic dream was particularly powerful. In the dream there was an esoteric group involved in a partnership endeavor, in which I was invited to participate. There was a banquet with many participants. The leader of the group sought me out to ask me a question. I was enthused to share with him but, as I began, he abruptly rose and walked away. I was puzzled and thought he was very rude. Then couples began forming a long line, and I was left on the other side of a glass door with no partner. I was heartbroken. I half-woke from this dream and became angry. Falling back into the dream, I said to the leader, "Do you think at my age I have all the time in the world to stand at the back of this line?" He replied, "You're not even in the line." Infuriated, I threw a dinner roll at him and left.

The scene changed and I was alone. Again, I half-woke, then fell back to sleep. I felt rejected, and then a voice said to me, "You rejected yourself." I realized I was responsible for the whole thing. In a flash I saw that I was all the players in the dream! So later in waking life, I asked myself why, in the beginning part of the dream, I (as the leader in the group) took the trouble of asking myself (as the seeker) a question and then abruptly walking away without hearing the answer. I realized that I don't listen to myself. I start to engage in the process of understanding myself, and then I wander away before the process is finished. How rude of me! I (as the leader) lost interest in me (as the seeker), and failed to follow through. I deemed myself unworthy of my own attention, and never even queued up.

Another thing that jumped out at me from the dream was that I am the leader as well as the seeker. I'm the one in charge, the one with the power to bring about the changes I'm looking for. No one else can do that. I'm also the others who were present in the dream, who successfully found partners, so the potential is there. But to realize the potential, I would need to pay attention to myself, to my inner life, which I'm more than happy to share (because I was leaning forward in the dream, intent on sharing myself with "him"). But I've been less willing to value the sharing, and work with it to accomplish my ends. I need to take myself more seriously, to honor and value myself in this process. No unconscious wandering off! Stay focused! Be with myself. I need to feel and acknowledge my worthiness, my power, and give it the attention it deserves. And patience is required (as indicated by the long line), not my forte!

So during the dream I realized that the root of the problem was my feelings of unworthiness. In the dream I asked, "How do I heal the unworthiness?" In answer, the scene changed again. I was with Robin White Star, and she said, "Oh, we can heal that!" She rang a little bell, waving it around me, much like smudging. Then I woke up.

I've never been enthusiastic about ceremonies. Growing up in the Catholic Church in the 1950s, there was plenty of ceremony, but it was vacuous. I remember the priest pushing the altar boys around impatiently. He was anything but sincerely involved in the ceremony. He was more involved in his own pompous "arse."

Upon waking from the dream, I went to the altar I'd made in my bedroom. I lit the candle, picked up my own little bell and began ringing it around me, as in the dream. I sang a wordless song again and again, communing with Spirit and asking for healing. An affirmation formed in my mind: "I see and acknowledge my own worthiness, and the worthiness of all." I ended with "Mitakuye Oyasin" (Lakota for All Are Related or All My Relations).

West Direction

Touching the Divine Within

---

*"All you SpiritKeepers of the West, Come, Look this Way!
Thank you, Bear, for your medicine of going within for
discernment and healing.*

*Thank you, Big Cats – Jaguar, Panther and Cougar – for
showing us how to live in two worlds, the intangible, invisible
world and the physical world.*

*Thank you, Divine Feminine, lunar energy,
for your gifts of life, death and rebirth.*

*Thank you, Twilight, for that sacred time and place in between.
Be with us on our journey! Give us the strength to look deeply
within our hearts, welcoming our fears and hurts to sit with
us in order to be transformed.*

*Thank you, Otter, for your playfulness
and women's medicine."*
Wah Doh

Accepting the Intensity of Self-Scrutiny

A big part of this ceremony is listening to your heart and discerning the difference between your beliefs and the truths that are often hidden or entangled within the beliefs. In fact, this ceremony invites you to listen so well that you can truly put into words how you perceive yourself to be, who you are calling, what kind of relationship you want to be in, and how to be in the right place at the right time to connect with the one you have called and not some other. All of this takes a large commitment on your part to be honest with yourself, open your heart to receive, and become congruent in your thoughts, words and actions. But it is doable – simply by listening and heeding the messages that will come your way once you have made the commitment to connect with your Soul Companion. All along the way in this West Direction of going within to find your answers, you will be engaging with the in-depth process of winnowing; just as the chaff is winnowed from the grain, you will be separating the beliefs, limitations and lies you were taught from your innate truths.

After I requested this ceremony, it became clear to me that I was indeed asking for assistance to do the healing work I needed to do on myself so that I could be in a soul-centered relationship with my Soul Companion, whether it actually manifested in this lifetime or a future one. I was committed to doing the inner work and transformation no matter what. I couldn't put a time limit on it and that's the way it is with healing. It's arrogant and self-defeating to tell Great Spirit that our requests have to be answered in a certain way and in a certain time frame. Healing can manifest quickly, especially when we are living a congruent life; however, to do the necessary inner work, peeling the layers of dis-ease and disharmony from our spirits, takes as long as it takes. One of my favorite teachings is "Don't give up before the miracle occurs." Persistence, tenacity, faith and trust all create a vibration of inner freedom that welcomes healing and transformation without limitations into our lives.

Several years ago, Veronica came to me to begin the process of calling her Soul Companion. Veronica had never had a boyfriend and didn't want to "waste" time on a casual dalliance; she wanted to be in relationship with "the one." We talked at length about what it means to call for a Soul Companion, and she said she wanted that kind of deep soul connection. She began the preparations of self-reflection, looking at her beliefs, sorting out the truths, facing some of her shadow material (all those qualities that we were taught it's not okay to be). She had never dreamed she would have to look at herself so closely. She was doing good work. Then, when Veronica's spirit helpers started showing her it was time for her to sort through her feelings and beliefs inherited from her parents and her culture, she balked. She finally said to me in a small voice, "This is too much work – I only want a boyfriend!" I laughed and said, "No, that's not the journey you requested and have begun, but if you want to stop and pursue a boyfriend rather than going forward with the Ceremony to call your Soul Companion, that's fine. It is totally up to you." Veronica is a beautiful young woman, intelligent and open-hearted, and she decided not to continue the ceremony. There is nothing wrong with that. It is always your choice as to how deep you want to dive into self-awareness and personal growth. She is doing what she needs to do, the way she needs to do it, and I support her all the way. The idea of a Soul Companion can be appealing, until we see the level of self-reflection and honesty required and the willingness needed to make changes in our habits, choices and lifestyle. And if it becomes unappealing at any point, that's okay. It's okay not to be ready. That means your journey of being in relationship will unfold in a different way. All journeys are "right." Some look easier than others, until they aren't. No matter which route we choose in life, we will learn what we need to learn – unless we stay asleep and numb to life, simply going through the motions of what is deemed socially acceptable and expected of us.

How many of you have had the experience of learning more quickly through adversity – it's a steeper climb, without as many water breaks, but it's a fast way to get where you want to go. Adversity certainly focuses our attention. Whether it's the loss of a job or the end of a relationship, an injury or illness, or other hardship, we often realize after the fact that it was the best thing that could have happened to us because it created an opportunity to surrender the way we thought we had to live our life to a different way that engaged our heart and soul to a greater degree. It created the means for internal growth and maturity. I'm grateful for the hardships I have experienced in my life. Like an arrow shot from a bow, each hardship sent me to the next leg of my journey with just a bit more clarity about myself and with greater skill in navigating through my life. I have no regrets because all those learning lessons helped me grow into the person I am today. And, because of all these life lessons, I am now quite clear that I want to live my life with grace and ease, without drama and trauma. According to Eckhart Tolle, "Suffering is necessary until you realize it isn't." Oh yeah!

Eventually we no longer see-saw from a state of being asleep, to being awakened by hardship, to falling back asleep. Rather, we are able to maintain our equilibrium in the middle way of being awake, present in the moment and listening to our inner Orendas. Even though we sometimes trip over our ego with the help of the tricksters Coyote and Rabbit, we are still willing to take the actions – inner and outer – that keep our momentum and trajectory on a true course of living life as a Sacred Human Being. That is what we are invoking through inner reflection, the catch and release of our beliefs and the naming of our truths. And once our spiritual muscles become fit, it doesn't feel like hard work. The intentional journey feels joyous, liberating, empowering and natural.

INVITING FEAR TO COME ALONG

We have talked quite a bit about the fears that we have been carrying around with us – sometimes for lifetimes – and how fear short-circuits the ability to live our life from our heart. Fear is a core energetic resonance that underlies all other resonances. In other words, every blockage or hurt we experience in life stems from a fear. Fear of the unknown, fear of separation, or fear of death are different ways of saying the same thing – that the ego mind cannot fathom not existing and will do everything in its power to make our choices based on its limited, physical perspective. We know that, as energetic Beings of Light, we cannot be created or destroyed. We just exchange form for formlessness and back again, in a never-ending spiral, while enrolled in this school we call Planet Earth. To not exist or not be is simply not possible because we are pure energy. This isn't true of the ego mind that does cease to exist at what we call death – when the soul lets go of the body, allowing it to break down into its basic physical elements.

Because fear is a natural component of our physical existence, it does no good to push it away, which is what we almost always attempt to do in an effort to overcome it. We see fear as an enemy that must be vanquished, again and again, no matter how often it rises from the dead. As long as we look at fear as something alien to us, we will be controlled by it – in its grasp – either by succumbing to it (which creates feelings of hopelessness, unworthiness, guilt and shame) or engaging in battle with it (which creates stress, battle fatigue, violence and a kill mentality). It takes a huge amount of energy to keep fear locked up, out of sight and out of mind. However, fear always finds a way to escape – the guards grow weary, the door is accidentally left unlocked because we weren't paying attention, or a circumstance in life triggers its release. Then we are once again succumbing or fighting and using energy that could best be used for problem-solving and for the expression of our life purpose.

There is another option that actually heals the spirit and returns balance and peace to the mind, as well as the body. It involves having a dialogue with fear, whenever it gets our attention. We can invite fear to come along with us in our life. Rockingbear taught me to talk to my fear. Invite my fear to come along, telling it I'm doing whatever it's fearful about anyway, but it is welcome to come along for the ride. I'm still in the driver's seat and fear can sit in the back. By inviting my fear along, it is my guest and has an active role to play (as a guest) and loses its power over me. I initiate the engagement and let it know what it can and can't do. At first – like any other undeveloped part of ourselves – it will test the limits or parameters we have set. So keep the invitation simple and issue it as many times as you need to.

When I was a young girl I loved to sing. Without even being aware of it, I would often sing when I was playing outside. One day when I was around 10, unbeknownst to me, a neighbor lady heard me singing and told my mom I had a beautiful voice and would probably want to take voice lessons to unfold it to a greater degree. My mom was understandably proud about the comment and relayed it to me, asking me if I wanted voice lessons. I was appalled that someone had heard me sing and I grew very shy. I didn't want voice lessons and I didn't sing outside any longer. I continued singing in chorus because we didn't have to do solos. Even thinking about singing by myself in front of people would cause my heart to pound and my breath would grow short. As a young adult, I gave talks and lectures, sometimes in front of hundreds of people, and had no problem – as long as I didn't have to sing. I wrote many songs and picked out their melodies on a guitar. I loved the group singing we did in the Inner Peace Movement, and I continued singing but only when alone in the house or in the car. Also, because it was fun making up lullabies for my baby son, I would sing to him all the time.

Well, there came a day in my training with Rockingbear that I received teachings about medicine songs. A medicine song or chant is an ally to a healer. Singing a song or chant increases energy when needed for healing, reaffirms the connection to Spirit before more difficult shamanic tasks, and feeds the holy by inviting the Medicine Ancestors to participate in ceremony. I had heard Rockingbear's personal medicine song that he sang before certain healing work, and I was familiar with other ceremonial songs sung by elders in the Arapaho Little Boys and Little Girls Sweat Lodge Ceremony and around the fire at the Vision Quest Ceremonies. Rockingbear suggested that it was time for me to listen for my personal medicine song and I was eager to discover it. I lit a fire at home, offering cedar and my gratitude to the fire and to my medicine song for showing itself to me and then sat in the darkness, open and willing to receive. Each time a note or sound came into my mind, I would give it voice (I made sure I was alone!). I used my turtle rattle to accompany me. Repetitive patterns started to emerge through vocables – sounds that have no meaning but can be replicated. As I sank further into the thrall of my song, all of its notes, inflections, and sounds became crystal clear to me. My song had revealed itself to me! I kept it close and didn't share it at first. I asked Rockingbear how I could use this medicine song since I was too fearful to sing in front of others. He told me, "Invite your fear to come along. Let it know you are going to sing this song anywhere and at any time it's needed. It's welcome to be a witness, but you are going to do it anyway, whether it comes along or not."

Then, at the fire at Vision Quest that year I heard a prompting from my ancestors to sing my song. I had been inviting my fear to come along for several months, and so, determined to sing, I took a deep breath, closed my eyes, and ...out came a squeak and then several more. I was trembling so hard, and my throat was so tight, not much could come out. I took another breath and now a little bit of my song came out. Then I was done. It was all I could do that first time. It was late at night with only a few people around the fire. All had listened respectfully and made no comment. So bit by bit, with support from my Monday Night circle members, I began to trust my voice, calling in the directions with my medicine song when requested.

One day, Usha asked me if I would sing at her engagement ceremony before the directions were called in. I was honored and terrified. It would be a large gathering of the community and many had never heard me sing. I continued to invite my fear to come along with me because I was singing whether it was there or not. As we gathered and people were still taking their seats, I thought I would practice in my mind and I found that I couldn't remember it, my mind was blank. I had to really hunker into my power and comfort myself with the knowledge that my medicine song would be there when I needed it. Usha welcomed everyone and then it was my turn to sing. I started playing my rattle and there, deep within me, my song emerged and I was able to give it voice.

I now sing other songs, most notably the Cherokee Eagle Song which I sang at Rockingbear's Celebration of Life ceremony. It's rare that I need to invite my fear to come along with me, although I usually close my eyes to sing which helps me to stay centered.

Fear has mostly grown tired of traipsing around after me and no longer has the intensity and power it once held.

I have used this healing method an untold number of times with numerous fears and, each time I do, the hold that fear has over me diminishes and is replaced with joy, the true expression of my soul. Am I still fearful? Yes, sometimes. This is ongoing work for a lifetime. But with each invitation, fear becomes my ally, no longer strong enough to paralyze me or stop me from being myself.

As you discover the fears and limitations that come up for you when contemplating a relationship with your Soul Companion, please take a moment to invite those fears to come along with you as you delve into the inner clearing work that's needed at this time. We all have fears that try to stop us from achieving our heart's desire. The key is realizing that we are not our fears, they are simply part of the ego mind that can be invited to come along on this grand adventure of calling your Beloved. Whether it's fear of being vulnerable, fear of losing yourself, fear of being happy, or any of the thousand other faces that fear wears from time to time, remember that you are the driver and Great Spirit is the navigator and all other energies in the back seat are there by your invitation.

BECOMING CLEAR ABOUT WHAT YOU WANT

As I prepared for the Calling Ceremony, I had been single for almost twenty years, after marrying young at 19 and divorcing 7 years later. Along the way I had the usual assortment of boyfriends, lovers and dates, but no serious, long-term relationship had developed in all that time. I had wondered if I was capable of sustaining a long-term commitment or if I was able to truly love another adult human being in an intimate, authentic way. I loved my family and my friends and experienced rich relationships with them, so why wasn't I experiencing the kind of deep, loving relationship I yearned for with a man? I had tried all the usual "advice" of attracting a mate, read lots of books, and talked endlessly with my girlfriends who were in the same situation (even some who were married at the time, but still felt the same yearnings I was articulating). I went to social functions (museum openings, art shows and festivals), I went out dancing with friends, and I had working relationships with single men that I wished would transcend the workplace, but it never happened. The men who were interested in me I variously labeled "too boring, too old, too young, or too out of touch with their inner life" and, of course, the ones who made my heart go pitter-patter were oblivious to my charms. So what was blocking me? What was stopping me from making the deep connection I desired? Something was certainly missing. Some key element of my personality or psyche wasn't open to making a deep connection with a man. Fear, distrust, judgments, limitations and stereotypical thinking all acted as barriers. I knew I needed to do more self-examination to clarify what was going on inside of me and what I needed to do to change my life.

I had read that if you look too hard for love, are too "desperate," love is going to be elusive, but if you concentrate on other parts of your life, then it will eventually sneak up on you and smack you right on the lips! So "Okay," I thought, "I can do that." In fact, a period of not seeking would give me an opportunity to do the needed work on myself, to get my head clear and my heart untangled from a past hurtful, and not unusual, emotionally perilous love life. I had always been a rather independent person, head-strong and self-sufficient, so I began my campaign of being comfortable as a single woman. I didn't need a partner to feel complete. I didn't need a man in my life to feel loved. I was happy with my life and with myself. I was working two jobs, eventually buying my first home, and sharing my life with 3 feline companions. I didn't need a partner to validate me, stroke me (emotionally and physically) to convince me that I was loveable. I lived with these thoughts and feelings until, low and behold, I was thirty-five! Uh-oh. Five years had gone by since this great campaign was put in motion. But after all this time, I still wanted a partner, damn it, with all my heart and soul!

Now it was time to make some choices in my life because I wanted to be a mother, too. I couldn't keep waiting and since no one was on the dance floor with me, or waiting in the wings or even on the horizon, I decided to become a single mother by choice. It was the best decision I ever made. I didn't know how this was going to happen or who would assist me with the miracle of life since that was the one thing I couldn't do all by myself, but I felt a power bigger than myself embrace this heartfelt choice of mine and I knew it would happen. Somehow, somewhere and with the right "someone." And it did, but that's a story for another time.

Now, with my son turning 7, it was time to choose again. For a long time, I had practiced being happy with my life just the way it was – being a single mom and a sister and a daughter. I accepted that if I lived my life without a Soul Companion, I would be just fine. I would continue to work on myself, growing and evolving in my spiritual growth, still loving and living to the best of my ability. I practiced being willing to accept what I couldn't change in my life. But in those dark middle-of-the-night hours, when I was truly honest with myself, I had to admit that I still wanted to be a part of a couple, to be in relationship with my Beloved. I was yearning for companionship on the soul level.

It was time to manifest another miracle. It was time to make the choice that I was ready and willing to take any and all actions and non-actions to bring my dream to fruition. Even if it didn't materialize in this lifetime, I was still willing to put energy behind my dream. I made a clear intention to myself and my ancestors, to my spirit guides, and to the Cosmos, that I wanted to go through the rest of my life with a Soul Companion. I wanted that challenge and experience, that level of engagement in my life. I wanted to delve into the shadow parts of myself that can only be revealed by being in an intimate, authentic relationship. I was scared to death. I had no idea if I could hold my center of gravity and keep living and working with the level of consciousness I had attained for myself while being in an authentic, intimate relationship. In the past I was always knocked off my pivot point when in relationship, unable to stay in my power.

But I had never felt as solid, as clear and strong as I did after sitting in circle with Rockingbear for several years. I finally reached the point where I could honestly say, "I'm ready. I've done lots of inner work. I understand how to better live my life with impeccability, to live my life with clarity, to live my life with love, compassion and personal power. And I'm willing to continue doing the work on myself as I manifest this dream." I didn't know for sure that I would be able to maintain all of these achievements while being in relationship, but I knew I wanted the opportunity to find out. Now, after being in relationship with my Soul Companion since 2001, I can say that on the whole I have been able to stay in my personal power, to maintain my inner balance, and to express my true feelings. Surprisingly, it's been far easier than I ever dreamed possible. Easier because we are heart connected and have made agreements with each other to be respectful, honest, supportive and live our lives without drama. In fact, I've been able to be more of who I truly am because of being in a relationship that totally supports all aspects of my life. It has enriched my life to a degree I had not thought possible.

My partner, my Soul Companion, is as open, willing and committed to being in an authentic, intimate relationship as I am. We choose to walk beside each other as equals – sometimes leading, sometimes following, and sometimes walking abreast. When my life gets tough for me, I'm grateful for his hand that helps me keep my footing. And I am just as willing to help him at those times when I am the more sure-footed one. I'm talking about being in balance, within ourselves and in relationship with each other as Soul Companions. It's possible. It's real. And it's a work in progress.

ATTRIBUTES, VALUES, AND THE ESSENCE OF WHAT'S IMPORTANT

Here's an important question, "What gender suit does your Soul Companion wear in this lifetime?" Discerning whether you wish to be relationship with a man or a woman (however that label is worn by an individual) is a fundamental choice to make as you begin your calling. Being willing to be true to yourself, and honest with the Fire, ensures that your heart-connected Beloved is ready and willing to be in a relationship with you. Usually the choice is obvious, as we know ourselves pretty well, but sometimes there are nuances that have to be explored to gain the clarity necessary before sitting with the Fire to make our call.

Ted had known he was gay from an early age and was only interested in being with a man. As he took an inventory of his recent, past relationships, he acknowledged that the last two men to whom he was attracted were straight men. These men were willing to be friends, although he desired more. Ted had put all his energy into these relationships, hoping that one of them would work out. Finally, after looking at his beliefs about himself that had to do with shame, self-worth and self-respect, he replaced those beliefs with the truth that now resonated within him: that he was loveable and worthy of an intimate, loving, sexual relationship with a man who fully and completely desired the same.

Melanie had grown children from her first marriage with a man, been divorced for many years, and had most recently been in same-sex relationships, having fully identified as a lesbian. She had spent quite a few years on her own, intentionally dancing with solitude and aloneness in order to do some major inner clearing and lineage healing work. When Melanie discerned it was time to call a Soul Companion into her life, she was asked to be clear about who she was calling. As she dropped into her Orenda, visualized her future, and opened her heart, she realized it could be a man or a woman. The gender was not important so long as they had all the qualities and attributes she was looking for in a partner. She continued her calling from this awareness, remaining open to whomever answered her call.

My teachers taught me that Creator holds no judgments regarding same-sex, transgender, or non-sexual relationships, or any other form of self-identification, so long as the relationships are consensual and enhance our self-respect rather than diminish it. Creator and all of Creation have no need to hold judgments or mete out punishments; we humans do that so often and so well all on our own! The Calling Ceremony invites you to examine the beliefs you hold about your gender, your body, and your ability to love and be loved in emotionally and spiritually healthy and life-affirming ways, without judgment, guilt, self-hatred or punishment. This is life-changing work. To fully accept yourself as a Divine expression of Creation, with all your quirks and weaknesses, as well as your powers, talents and abilities, is to live your life in its purest, highest form. Entering into the Calling Ceremony creates an opportunity to bravely live a more authentic and fulfilling life.

Now, per Rockingbear's instructions, I made a comprehensive list of the qualities and attributes I was looking for in the man that I was inviting into my life. Prior to the Calling Ceremony, I had made several attempts at making these lists, each one becoming more specific but less limiting that the preceding ones. I know many of you have also made lists before to no avail. The most important aspect of this work is to be specific, intentional, and conscious of the attributes and qualities, without being limiting. For example, to say we want a partner who earns $100,000 a year is extremely limiting to Spirit. Remember, we are co-creating this ceremony with Great Spirit and need to accept that we will receive all that we ask for and more, as all the forces in the Universe mobilize and conspire to assist us. When we are limiting in our request we effectively cut off that assistance. It's telling Spirit the way it has to be, leaving no room for magic, for grace. Saying that we want a partner who is financially solvent, abundant, or fiscally responsible, without attaching specific monetary values, are all ways to be specific without being limiting regarding their financial health.

So this time I was quite specific in my lists of traits and qualities, without limiting Great Spirit in any way. I found myself breaking the list into categories to better define my desires: Spiritual, Emotional, Mental, and Physical. I also included a separate listing of the major qualities I did not want in my partner. These, of course, had been gleaned from my past and, sometimes, disastrous relationships, including my first marriage. I kept checking in with Rockingbear as I was creating these lists of what I wanted, what I didn't want, and what I was willing to do and to release for this relationship to come into my life. With his insight and wisdom, I was able to hone the attributes and qualities most important to me until I felt a completeness, a clarity and a congruence of my heart and mind. I have included these lists to serve as a guide for your own foray into transforming your desires, wants and needs into the specific attributes and qualities you desire in your Soul Companion. As you will see, these lists were works in progress, messy and quite childlike. I made a point of not rewriting them to make them "perfect." It was my way of getting out of my head and expressing what was in my heart and soul.

After I listed the traits and qualities in each category, I looked for the common vibration so I could hold all my intentions in one key word. The key word that summed up the physical attributes I was looking for was "physically balanced." Emotionally, I wanted a mature man. A man who had done his inner work along the way to heal the hurts of his past, or "emotionally healthy." Mentally, I wanted a man who was able to process information and take action in his life by accessing his analytical, fact-oriented 'left brain' and his feeling, relational-oriented 'right brain' which I summed up as "whole-brained." And, most importantly, I wanted him to be "spiritually awake."

What I did not want in the man coming into my life was for him to be "asleep" – unaware of who he was, where he was going and how to live his life in a good way as a Sacred Human Being. What I was willing to do was to "receive love," opening my heart to an intimate relationship, accepting my partner as a divine being, worthy of my love. I was willing to be loved unconditionally by my Soul Companion, both in his words and his actions. What I was willing to give up in my life so that I could be in this intimate, authentic relationship with my Beloved was "fear" – fear of being unlovable, fear of true intimacy, fear of being vulnerable, fear of losing control of my life.

I started with the following typewritten list, adding qualities and attributes as I thought of them. Later I honed the list, breaking it up into different categories and making it more of a work of art so I could energetically hold the information more clearly. These are offered as examples, a way to spark your imagination – whatever works for you is the right way for you to discern and describe the person with whom you want to be with in this soul companion relationship.

QUALITIES AND ATTRIBUTES I WANT IN MY HUSBAND

1. He is balanced between his male and female energies

2. He is spiritually aware and awake

3. He has a loving, open heart

4. He discerns energy, people and situations and takes appropriate action or non-action

5. He is sophisticated and down-to-earth

6. He lives in two worlds easily - physical, material and spiritual, energetic

7. He wants to and is capable of loving one woman, creating a close family feeling and home

8. He loves me with all his heart and soul

9. I love him with all my heart and soul

10. He easily takes care of himself and shares generously with his loved ones

11. He is physically active, likes to hike, dance, walk and swim

12. He is in good health, has good eating habits, is vegetarian or respects and supports Indigo and I in our eating habits

13. He is intelligent, well read, inquiring mind, curious and a good conversationalist

14. He laughs easily, smiles nicely, good teeth and twinkle in eye when joking or amused

15. He is kind, compassionate, able to give and receive in balance and when appropriate

16. He enjoys animals, wants a pet like a cat, rabbit or others

17. He is interested in organic gardening, flowers, trees and plants

18. He likes to work with his hands to build, repair and create

19. He likes his work, finds it interesting but has other interests of equal importance

20. He loves Indigo and wants to be his father and friend - he feels comfortable with my child rearing practices and complements me in helping Indigo become a fine adult man

21. He gets along easily with my family and I get along easily with his family

22. I feel comfortable, secure and the best that I can be with him

23. He feels confortable, secure and the best that he can be with me

24. There is high sexual chemistry between us, passionate, easy and fun - meets my physical and emotional needs and I meet his

25. He loves to kiss, is romantic and understanding of the feminine

26. He earns well and is comfortable with money, saves and invests and spends with equal aplomb

27. He is an interesting person, special is some very obvious way

28. He utilizes his talents and supports me in utilizing mine

29. Physically, he is of average height, attractive with long hair and fit

30. He is spontaneous, flexible, good-natured and loves life

31. He is honest; his thoughts, words and actions are impeccably the same

32. We have a strong attraction and commitment to each other, spiritually, physically, emotionally and mentally

33. He is willing to be vulnerable, open and intimate and continue evolving in a loving, intimate relationship

34. He respects life and recognizes that his decisions effect the next seven generations

35. He is attuned to his real feelings and expresses his feelings easily and appropriately

36. He is affectiona*te, demonstrative,* likes to hold hands, hug and be physically close

37. He respects me as a mother, a woman, a wife and a person

38. He trusts my judgment, my decisions and my inner knowings

39. He is interested in Native American spirituality, dreamtime and spiritual experiences

40. He wants to and is capable of protecting me and cherishing me when I need and/or ask for his protection and caring

Authentic / Intimate / Monogamous / Long-term
Relationship with Physical Man.
Loving.

I DESIRE.

Physical -
Healthy, Attractive, Good skin & teeth.
Strong, listens to his body
Sensual, playful loves to kiss, hug, touch
  + be touched.
Sexually mature + passionate
Great smile - lights up his eyes.
Non-Smoker
No drugs
Light drinker
Eats healthy nutritious foods / organic
Lives in balance / respect for environment,
  nature, creatures
Mechanically inclined, good w/ hands
Financially secure, grounded, abundant-
Does work he loves
Balanced lifestyle between work + personal
Shares his abundance with Indigo + me
Has one child - boy or girl around
  or children
Indigo's age - child(ren)/are healthy emotionally
  + spiritually awake

BALANCED

Authentic/Intimate/Monogamous/Long-term
Loving
Relationship with Physical Man.

I DESIRE

<u>Emotionally</u> — To cherish me
    Gentle, loving, compassionate, strong
    Understanding, honorable, integrity
    Respects/honors the Feminine
    Capable of emotional intimacy
    Wants authentic, intimate relationship
    Honest, direct, secure
    Open heart to give + receive love
    Loves me wholeheartedly
    Loves Indigo w/ no reservations
    Healthily protective of Indigo + me
    Comfortable with + not threatened by my
        close family relationship
    Communicates + discerns feelings, wants,
     needs + desires easily + appropriately
    Balanced + healthy.
    Worked through issues w/ Mother/Father
    Comfortable w/ silence
    Socially adept   HEALTHY

Authentic/ Intimate /Monogamous /Long term/
Loving Relationship w/ Physical Man

I DESIRE

Mentally
    Intelligent
    Disciplined
    Positive
    Discernment
    Computer savvy
    Alert
    Inquisitive
    Humorous
    Achieves goals w/ease + grace
    Makes informed choices
    Uses both sides of brain
    Well- educated
    Creative
    Open-minded - explore new ideas/thoughts

            WHOLE - BRAINED

Authentic/Intimate/Loving/Monogamous/
Longterm Relationship w/ Physical Man.
                    I DESIRE

Spiritually
Supportive of each other's work/purpose
Awake + aware
Knows, communicates clearly + listens to
    his guides, teachers + protectors.
Impecabble
Respects/honors Native/Earth Spirituality
Knows himself - wise
~~unblock healing~~
Healer
Joy, love, creativity + healing
    generated for us + others by our
    being together
Teachers to each other
Attuned to Indigo + his purpose
Supportive of Indigo's work + purpose
Adept at going within - meditation/ journeys
            AWAKE

Authentic/Intimate/Loving/Monogamous/
Longterm Relationship w/ Physical Man.

WHAT I AM WILLING TO DO
Let go of fear
Open my heart to love

Be accepting of myself + my body

Be secure in my ability to be loved

Be vulnerable, not in control all the time
Surrender to relationship.

Be loving, mindful + gentle
~~Spend~~ time with him

Create an opening in my heart, mind +
life for him

Be honest, impeccable, authentic, playful

Be sensitive to be in the right place
at the right time to ~~find~~ each other

To receive love
Be appreciative of him

RECEIVE LOVE

Authentic/ Intimate/ Loving / Monogamous
Longterm Relationship w/ Physical Man

<u>WHAT I DON'T WANT</u>

judgmental of me, my body or my lifestyle
Jealous of my relationship w/ Indigo or family
Competitive
Cynical
Manipulative
Victim Energy
Fear based
Insensitive
Needing to prove himself to me or Others or
himself.
Walking wounded
Addictive personality
Low self-esteem
On the edge financially.
Out-of-balance

ASLEEP

Authentic / Intimate / Loving / Monogamous /
Long term Relationship w/ Physical Man.

Calling Ceremony

Be open - receptive
Listen / see / Know / feel
Engage / Dialogue / Explore
Discern
Choose   Felt turtle nearby
Commit   Facing the fire
                and my altar
Time table   Went through the
Actions   fire and sat on the other side.
                Tremendous heat and light
Welcome   from the fire and the sun.

Several weeks ago   Saw sand and the water in
after I requested   the distance. Drum was
the calling I dreamed   powerful. Magnetized me.
of a man - saw   Gift I gave him - macaw feather
his high school   Gift he gave me - a wolf skin
picture - brown   and a white flower.
hair / eyes + smile
lit up   (MAKE MY DESIRES KNOWN)
his eyes.
Day before heard   ) OFFER (Let him know where
the name David   )   (I would be - where
              (TRANSFORM)   he could find me.
                             Name of Michael came
                             to me.

Date Set: 11/31/00   SO BE IT

BALANCE OF FEMININE AND MASCULINE

Did you know that each female body carries 51% feminine genes and 49% masculine? And of course, male bodies carry 51% masculine genes and 49% feminine. We are closer to being androgynous than to being either all female or all male. Men and women are more alike than we are different. It's only this small difference of 2% that makes each of the genders so attractive, magnetizing, and unfathomable to the other! This is the wisdom of Yin and Yang – equal but different, each offering unique strengths, abilities, talents AND weaknesses. Problems arise when we look to the "other" to complete us, to provide all the attributes that we lack. Some call this a co-dependent relationship and it cannot sustain itself in the long run. It isn't nor can it be that black and white. We must each become whole and healed within ourselves so that we can give and receive from a balanced center point. If we are continually out of balance, leaning on our partner for more than 50% of our emotional/spiritual support, or pulling the other off their pivot point with our demands, drama and pain, we will see the relationship start to seesaw wildly, until it topples or implodes, sending emotional debris in all directions. Not only are we wounded again, but our friends and relatives are often hurt by the fallout as well.

When we get caught up in stereotypes and labels pertaining to our feminine and masculine natures – nurturing belongs to women, aggressive behavior to men, women are indecisive, men aren't willing to talk about their feelings, to name a few – we limit the full emotional ranges that are our natural birthright. These stereotypes might fit some women and some men some of the time, but not all women and all men all of the time. It's an absurd, emotional dead end. That's what makes standup comedy so funny – it zeroes in on some stereotype that we all relate to, to one degree or another. But to live our life from the perspective of these limiting stereotypes is the way of madness, dysfunction, and destruction – personally and collectively – which we see far too often.

In *Body Metaphors – Releasing God-Feminine in Us All*, Genia Pauli Haddon articulates an understanding of the complete balance within oneself which I'll paraphrase here. Namely, that the feminine carries two energies: the nurturing, caring, holding and embracing one (womb), and the exertive, action-oriented, out in the world one (breasts). Likewise, the masculine carries the spontaneous, active, clearly defined one (penile) and the embracing, holding and nurturing one (testicular). This way of looking at the totality of each gender was so helpful to me as I embarked on my feminine journey. I became clear that I could possess a balance *within* my feminine and later, I became clear that I wanted to be in relationship with a man who possessed a balance *within* his masculine. Whether we or our partners identify as male, female or transgender, this awareness of inner balance is a foundational piece on which to create a healthy union with our Soul Companion.

To further illustrate this point, Rockingbear shared about a time when he comforted a small child who had fallen down in front of him. As he consoled him and helped him to his feet, the mother came rushing over, thanking him. She remarked that it was wonderful to see a man so in touch with his inner feminine that he would comfort a child like he did. Rockingbear was amazed that she equated nurturance, care and comfort only with the feminine. He had done a lot of inner work to be in balance between his masculine and feminine and within his masculine and feminine energies, but she was attempting to limit his masculine response through stereotyping. He shared that the masculine has the same inherent ability and desire to nurture, care and comfort as the feminine, most likely in slightly different ways, but with the same effect. This is an important understanding to have for ourselves as we become more clear about who we are and who we want to be with in relationship. Women, of course, often experience stereotyping. A common example is a woman being called "bossy," "cold," "a bitch," or "a ball-buster" in leadership situations, even though they are using the same words, leadership styles or business criteria as a man. Balance is the key – within ourselves and within our relationships. Only then can we truly express ourselves as Sacred Human Beings.

BEING SPECIFIC WITHOUT BEING LIMITING

When we clearly state what we want, all the forces of the Universe mobilize to bring that into physical reality. The more clearly we have discerned and defined our request, the more likely we will want what we receive. Remember the old adage, "Be careful what you ask for because you'll get it!" This has happened to me numerous times. When I realized that I got *exactly* what I asked for and it wasn't what I wanted, I learned that I had to be more specific. Being specific means we have distilled our desire, our prayer, our request to its essence. No frills or distractions. "Just the facts, Ma'am." This is the bottom line truth for us.

We limit our request when we say it has to be done by a certain time, in a certain way, with a certain person, in a certain city or part of the country. We can put so many conditions on our request that it is too heavy to take flight.

And know this: whatever we are not willing to do in order for that request to come about, that is what will be asked of us. For instance, when we request a new job and are very specific about what this job looks like and we also say it can't be in the city where our in-laws live, the odds are very good that the only job that fits our request will be in that city. Spirit has a great sense of humor, laughing at us, not with us! In the Native teachings, this is called Coyote Medicine – when our ego tricks us into looking like a fool because we're not being authentic. Another trickster, Rabbit, will dig under the roots on our path so that we trip over our ego and go sprawling – usually in front of the very ones we wish to impress. These two medicine ways help us to laugh at ourselves and not take our silliness and prejudices so seriously. In this way, we can shift the focus from our ego-mind to our heart-mind and begin to live as Sacred Human Beings instead of scared human beings. If we don't make the shift into our heart-mind, our requests will be watered down by the limitations of the ego-mind so that nothing happens – staying in the realm of wishful thinking and wouldn't it be nice if . . ..

Also, since our brains don't actually process negatives, but simply hear the rest of the message, it is critical that we state our requests in the positive. For example, "I don't want to be in a relationship with an emotionally immature person" becomes "I want to be in a relationship with an emotionally immature person." Scary, isn't it? "Don't run in the street" is interpreted as "run in the street." Negatives become unintended messages that confuse and thwart our ability to move in new directions. State everything in the positive and you will see your requests fulfilled, changes will come about in miraculous ways and you will move forward with grace and ease. Making requests specific without being limiting is an art form and practice is absolutely necessary until it becomes internalized.

I have learned from my teachers that requests are not answered because we "earn" them or "deserve" them – racking up enough gold stars, brownie points or badges on our sash, cashing them in like so many green stamps. Our requests are answered because we are powerful beings of light. It is our right as beings of light to co-create with Great Spirit. Every force in the Universe, Cosmos, God, Great Spirit, Divine Light – whatever you wish to call it – mobilizes and conspires to assist us. We can also call this force Love. Remember, Love is an action, not simply a feeling. The vibration or frequency of Love is our connection to all the beings in the Universe. Because we are Love, our requests manifest in the most miraculous ways, ways that go beyond the left brain's attempt to orchestrate or logically figure things out. Just as we love a child and will move heaven and earth to fulfill their needs and desires, so too does the Universe love and help us. Grandfather Sun doesn't shine on you because you earned those life-giving rays, or because you have been deemed "good" or "worthy." Grandfather Sun shines on everyone alike with no judgment or distinction. It is our birthright – we don't have to earn it. In this same way, our requests are answered because we are a part of the Web of Life and co-creators of Life with Great Spirit. A request is the beginning of everything. If a request or prayer is specific without being limiting, then all the forces in the universe rally to bring that request into physical manifestation. If we stay with vague yearnings, wishful thinking or hopes, an actual request hasn't been made and no action is called forth. A request comes from the deepest place within us, our Orenda. When we are honest with ourselves about what we truly want – our innermost desires – we can clearly state that in the form of a request.

One time, a woman was driving up from Mexico to the North Carolina Vision Quest with one of Rockingbear's apprentices. She was talking about how excited she was to be questing (going up on the mountain for 4 days and 4 nights to seek a vision) – going on and on about how grateful she was for the opportunity. The apprentice was getting confused though because it became apparent that the woman really didn't understand what the Vision Quest Ceremony was all about and what it entailed to be a questor. He finally asked her point blank if she had made a tobacco request to Rockingbear to quest. When she answered in the negative, he grinned and said, "Oh, then you're just talking about it!"

When I was growing up, my family often went on vacation to Lake Erie, renting a powerboat so we could water ski. I have many fond memories of long days on the water, in the boat and on skis. Each time when we returned home, my parents would begin a familiar refrain, "One day we'll own a boat, motor and skis!" It never came about. It was a nice idea and we all became comfortable with the idea that we might have these things someday, far in the future. Actually turning that idea into a request and grounding it with actions (like a ski boat jar for our extra change or minimizing Christmas gifts to add to the fund) never occurred. I realized later that we didn't really know how to create the actions to support this desire so it stayed in the realm of wishful thinking. Making a formal request to Spirit is an action and an intention which begins magnetizing the energy to crystalize that request into the physical realm.

When prayers are answered and requests made manifest, it is routinely called luck, happenstance or coincidence. It is much more than that. In olden times, answered prayers were often labeled magic, sorcery or witchcraft, invoking fear and retribution. Requests made manifest is nothing to be afraid of nor should it be labeled as unnatural. It is simply a Universal Law that as a Being of Light, we create our life by inner, crystallized soul desire. This is how we migrate through our lives, with no two lives the same. Connections are forged in the Invisible World first, then manifested in the Visible World. Luck or synchronicity, magic or miracles, all are simply created through our thoughts, words and actions. This is the Web of Life – every being of the Planetary Family connected through an inner crystallization of who we each are in the present moment, shifting and realigning as we grow and evolve in consciousness. When our thoughts, words and actions are congruent, we are then aligned within ourselves. Our requests have power, clear purpose and absolute trust fueling them. In that moment of crystal clarity, our desire flashes through the Universe like a laser beam, igniting the Invisible Flame of Manifestation to bring that request into physical beingness, whether it is world peace, our Soul Companion, or the right cat sitter. No request is too small or too big.

DOMESTICATION

Personal likes and dislikes, prejudice, bigotry, fear and hatred are all part of what Rockingbear referred to as "domestication." Domestication for us two-leggeds is no different than what is employed to make animals and plants more compliant and human friendly. We have been taught since birth to live within the rights and wrongs, the rules and regulations, and the social mores and customs of the time and place in which we were born – either learning through punishment or rewards, or both. When our wild, indigenous soul is reined in and punished too harshly, our spirit can be broken and our imagination – that very real portal between the tangible, visible world and the intangible, invisible world – is squashed. We learn that it's okay and even necessary to compare ourselves to others, to compete with one another to prove our worth, and to judge ourselves and others as worthy or not (usually not). We begin to forget who we truly are – unique beings of light and love – and become docile, fearful, and unconscious of our soul's purpose. Pablo Picasso said, "Every child is an artist. The problem is how to remain an artist once he grows up." In Kindergarten all children raise their hand when asked if they are artists, but by 6th grade, only a few are brave enough to claim that title, mostly from fear of being judged not good enough. Many adults will flat out tell you they can't sing, dance, draw, heal, – just fill in the blank of whichever artistic or inner expression is being discussed – because, somewhere along the line, their unique expression wasn't deemed acceptable compared to some ideal held by society or within their family. Our task is to reclaim these lost energies by allowing ourselves to sing, dance, create art, make music, or heal without comparison or judgment – simply to the best of our abilities.

Being domesticated means we have forgotten that we are all unique expressions of the Divine and our gifts and talents are important and make a difference in our world. One woman who sat in Rockingbear's circle for many years related a story about her two sons. She happened to overhear a conversation that her firstborn (around age 4) was having with his new little brother – "Can you remind me what's it like where you came from? I'm starting to forget." We all have forgotten our true nature, to one degree or another, and need to remind each other of the truth through our words and actions. That's what a spiritual tradition or path is all about – the teachings and ceremonies help us to remember our true essence and move beyond whatever level of domestication exists within us. The wild, indigenous soul, innate within us, is not to be feared, even though it has been labeled "savage" or "not civilized." Untamed, wild horses aren't savages – they are free to be themselves. Once tamed, they do others' bidding – sometimes through love and an energetic connection, but most often through fear and acquiescence for survival's sake. Our indigenous, untamed self remembers how to live according to our soul's purpose – and it remembers the happiness and bliss generated from that freedom.

Rockingbear often spoke about being a "Sacred Human Being" living in two worlds at one time – the spiritual, energetic world and the physical world of matter. He taught me that traveling back and forth in my consciousness between these two worlds is very draining – it takes a lot of energy to do so – while living in both at the same time requires less energy output and makes life a lot simpler and more enjoyable. But how do we start living as a Sacred Human Being? If I become caught in the illusion that spirit and matter are a duality, I create a separation between the two which makes it impossible to be in both at the same time. Here's an illustration. In the linear model, which is what informs the western or nonindigenous mind, the two parts of a duality are assigned opposite ends of the spectrum. In the indigenous worldview, everything exists within a circle – the never-ending spiral of life.

If you want to truly understand how this works, you can practice with this exercise. Name a duality – could be past/future, good/bad, dark/light, positive/negative, spirit/matter or any other pair that comes to mind. Assign one part of the pair to each hand (i.e. "good" to the right hand and "bad" to the left) and hold your arms straight out to the side at shoulder height. Keep them up as you visualize the straight line that extends beyond each hand from your fingertips, moving the dualities farther apart from each other. Now, how long can you maintain this line? No matter how fit you are, eventually you'll tire and have to break the line. When that happens in life, we choose which one to hold and identify with – "I'm a bad boy" or "I'm a good girl." "I'm a spiritual seeker so I don't need to be concerned with my physical health." "I've done awful things so there's no light in me." We pick a label or seesaw back and forth between the opposite labels, thinking we have to be one or the other. This is the illusion of separation. When asked an either/or question, Rockingbear would always reply, "Yes!" When I'm asked if the healing needed is spiritual or physical, I reply, "Both – it's always both." Now, hold your arms out to the side again with the same duality. Curve your arms so they form a circle with your hands touching in front of you. Now the parts of that duality are right next to one another. Keeping the circle, allow your arms to rest in your lap. How long can you hold this pose? For a very long time – it's effortless. Every point along the circle is now accessible.

When I go into my inner, sacred space to sit in council with my spirit helpers and allies, my past sits to the left of me, my future on the right, and my present sits across the circle. All aspects of myself are there, available to me – the good, the bad and the ugly! I accept them all to the best of my ability so I can continue bringing those shadowy aspects of myself out of the dungeon to sit at the dinner table with me in all their undomesticated wildness. Sure, it's uncomfortable at first, but the gifts these parts of me bring to the table are priceless – creativity, inventiveness, knowledge, wisdom and the knowingness of how to keep my balance when riding those really intense learning waves in my life. Every day I remind myself that I am a Being of Light, channeling that energy into my physical body to engage in the lessons and adventures found here on Mother Earth. I am here to learn and grow and to remain aware, each and every moment, that I am a Sacred Human Being, as is each and every one of us.

CALLING FROM THE HEART, NOT THE MIND

Our mind (or ego) loves to makes requests which, in actuality, turn out to be demands, usually regarding the things we think we ought to do, or have to have, or should be doing in our life by the time we are a certain age or at a certain place in our career. These mind requests have nothing to do with the heart requests we have been talking about for the Calling Ceremony. Mind requests are like the decisions we make – logical, symmetrical, linear, but they don't engage our hearts. They often fall in line with what our parents wanted for us, or what society says is a good thing to do even though we don't feel any resonance with them. Either early on or later on, mind requests run out of steam, being shown for the illusions they are.

A man came to me for healing a few years back, feeling empty and unfulfilled in his life. Turns out he loved to tinker with vintage cars in his free time. That was his true love – working with his hands to rebuild the motors and interiors. Something about it engaged his heart and when he talked about his passion, his enthusiasm was real. Because his parents wanted him to be a doctor and he had the brains for it, that was the career he pursued which he ultimately found unfulfilling, although he was good at it. He knew he was helping people, but with his heart disengaged his work left him feeling empty. Left to his own devices he would have excelled as a happy and fulfilled vintage car mechanic – not exactly the status or income his parents wanted for him, but who knows where that path, carved by the desires of his heart, would have taken him?

We have learned to talk ourselves out of our heart desires, thinking they should only live in the realm of imagination or fairy tales. Yet, there are many examples of people who have followed their hearts, breached the do's and don'ts drilled into them as children and are now living their dreams. Listen to their stories. They can inspire you to do the same. We can all live our own fairytale. We may have learned beliefs that say we are not smart enough, lucky enough, well-connected enough, affluent enough, sacrificing enough, and on and on. These are the lies. These beliefs have nothing to do with the truth that we can live our lives guided and directed by our heart choices. Yes, it's scary sometimes but not as much as you'd think! I have found that it is more exciting than scary. It is profoundly engaging and rewarding to take responsibility for my happiness and to dream my life into being the life I want to wake up to each day.

There are people all around the world (and you may be one of them) making requests or prayers for peace, harmony, mutual respect and equality for every being on the planet. When enough people are making the same request, being specific and not limiting (i.e., that some people are not worthy of respect or, because of past actions, certain persons wouldn't be included in this vision of peace), then these dreams, these collective requests, will be made manifest through amazing and miraculous ways. This phenomenon was articulated by Ken Keyes, Jr. in his book *The Hundredth Monkey*. "When a certain critical number of minds achieves an awareness, this new awareness may be communicated from mind to mind. Although the exact number may vary, this Hundredth Monkey Phenomenon means that when only a limited number of people know of a new way, it may remain the conscious property of these people. But there is a point at which if only one more person tunes-in to a new awareness, a field is strengthened so that this awareness is picked up by almost everyone!" It appears to be instantaneous – that's the magic and wonder of this principle. We are co-creators of our lives and of our collective experience together in this time and place called Planet Earth in the 21st century. We cannot make a request and then sit by idly waiting for it to fall into our lap, however. Once the request has been made, our work is to listen, trust and pay attention so we can take the actions or non-actions that we are being called to take in order to birth our dreams.

HAVING THE LAST WORD

When I hear someone say something as a blanket statement of fact when it is really just a belief of theirs, I make sure I have the last word – with myself. It's extremely important that we monitor what goes into our ears, as that is what is processed through our psyche. If the statement isn't true for me, I say softly under my breath, "That's not true for me," so my ears hear my truth. It's not about telling the other person – it's not about them. It's about us having the final word with ourselves so we are clear about our truths.

My first writing group was just me and my friend Shawn. Another writer asked to join us, so the 3 of us met together. She shared how she was living in a cold attic, no money, no social life, so that she could write and that's what writers needed to do – suffer and sacrifice for their art. Both Shawn and I said at the same time, "That's not true for me." We actually said the words out loud, but she didn't even hear us, she was so busy justifying her belief. We both wanted to make sure our bodies and psyches didn't think we were accepting her version of reality. Most of us think it's no big deal what we let slide, but casual remarks and our acceptance of them when they aren't congruent with our truth carry immense power, often because they are casual and therefore slip under our conscious radar to interact directly with our psyche. Fortunately, it's never too late to let yourself know that something isn't true for you. Because time is a reality of the physical world only, whatever words have been heard by our ears can be reframed as soon as we realize the need to do so, whether it is in the next instant or decades later. In this way, we are working outside of time or, in essence, becoming masters of time.

This became apparent to me after I realized that a comment my sister made to me was still operating within me years later. She's 6 years older than me, has never been married and at the time when she made her comment, didn't have any children (she later adopted a baby girl from China – my beautiful and talented niece). I was married in my early twenties, divorced 7 years later and, at that time, in my late thirties, had given birth to a child as a single mother by choice. One day my sister and I were out together and she said, "You can't get married again until I get married since I'm older." I laughed and said, "Yeah, okay." Well, when I began my Calling Ceremony preparation, going within to see what beliefs needed to be ferreted out so I could do this ceremony from my truths, this memory popped up. I realized I had taken it to heart – holding that belief to be true. In many times and places this was the norm – the older siblings had to be married first, each one being married in turn. I rewired my vibration when I was able to say, "That's not true for me any longer. It's okay for me to be in relationship with my Soul Companion even if my sister is not in a personal relationship." Sounds simple, and it is, AND it makes all the difference. What beliefs and agreements have you casually accepted that need to be rescinded or restated?

In the *Medicine Cards*, one of the animal totems listed is Rabbit. Rabbit's medicine teaches us about fear – through the acronym "false evidence appearing real." This is the challenge – to sort out the false evidence held in our beliefs so we can truly see the truths that will guide us in our life and in our quest for relationship with our Soul Companion. Beliefs are handed down from generation to generation, tied to specific times and places. Some of the beliefs from the Middle Ages we find ludicrous, steeped in ignorance and fear. But one day, not so far in the future, many of our widely held beliefs may be looked upon in the same way. Let's look at some specifics.

When I began looking at my beliefs in regard to relationships, I had already been sorting through other beliefs – disentangling them from my truths. One of my beliefs (that I talk about in an earlier chapter) had to do with how difficult it was for me to finish anything, courtesy of my mother who started many projects but finished few. I held resentment, anger and fear about that – feeling that I was my mother's daughter in this area. I too, loved to start things but would grow bored and not finish them. I realized that this belief in my temperament and abilities was shaped by my family of origin and was not in accordance with my personal truth of who I am and what I am able to do. When I saw that this habit didn't need to be true for me just because it was for my mother, I began the road to freedom in this area. This was an important belief to look at because I didn't want to start the Calling Ceremony and not finish it. My truth is that I can start something, grow bored or realize that I no longer want to do it and choose to set it down without guilt or shame, or I can go through the hard parts of any project and finish it, not because I am afraid of someone else judging me or criticizing me for not completing the task, but because I want to. I took back my own power which resides in my choices and gave away the fears of being judged and found not good enough. That freedom released my creativity and personal power so I could envision my dreams with clarity and strength of purpose. I was no longer weighing down my dreams with the belief of not being good enough and the fear of failure. I was taking responsibility for my choices – my truths.

Another high-impact belief I had to work on centered around the notion that since I was a strong-willed, independent woman, I couldn't or shouldn't show any vulnerability – that would be weakness. The insights I gained from the teachings of *Walks Tall Woman*, the Clan Mother who teaches us how to walk our talk, enabled me to replace that belief with the truth that it is okay to be vulnerable, to be authentic, and to need help and support physically and emotionally. This was a huge step and one that I continued working on after I was in relationship with my Soul Companion. I kept falling asleep, going unconscious and had to be reminded by my partner that I was cutting him off, compartmentalizing and otherwise not being open and authentic. I was making unilateral decisions, unaware of how my choices were impacting my Beloved, keeping my own council which I was used to doing, not being open and honest with how I was feeling and what was going on in my world. It wasn't pretty – in fact, during the first couple of years together it was extremely painful whenever I fell back into this belief. Gradually, with the help of my partner, I became less comfortable with this belief. It began to feel unnatural, constrictive and disrespectful to myself and to him. Now, I usually notice if I'm leaning back into this belief and pull out of it on my own, and sometimes it's so sneaky that I need my partner or others close to me to hold a mirror so I can better see what I'm unconsciously doing. When they remind me of my agreement to be open and forthcoming, trusting and vulnerable, I can say, "That's true for me!" We all need reminding now and again to be true to the agreements and truths we have identified.

On a larger scale, let's examine a prevalent collective belief that involves my country: The United States of America. As a society we hold the belief that democracy is the best form of government and every country should be a democracy. Because of this belief, we find ourselves in a position where we are willing to kill people in other countries so that we can bring them democracy. How twisted, right? But that is the nature of unexamined beliefs – people can even be willing to die or kill for them. Wouldn't it be better to simply be an example, so others can make up their own minds?

When the Dalai Lama was asked if he felt hatred in his heart for the way the Chinese had driven him and other monks from Tibet, forcing them to live outside their homeland and killing many of those left behind, he answered that he was eager for the Chinese to leave Tibet so that he and others could return to their homeland and would do everything in his power to effect that change, but that he did not hate those who had perpetrated these violent acts because he would then be no different from his oppressors. He was able to stay in his truth rather than getting sucked into a belief of tit for tat, hating those who hate. We can all learn from His Holiness the Dalai Lama and from the teachings of Jesus Christ to hold the truth of love, compassion and forgiveness within our hearts in the face of fear, injustice, hatred and violence. We can stand in the power of our truths and allow them to guide our thoughts, words and actions.

This ferreting out of beliefs and disentangling them from the truths within us is extremely important work, whether you are doing the Calling Ceremony or not. It is a path of self-realization, a path to soul freedom. I invite you to begin the process of identifying the beliefs that no longer serve you, especially as it pertains to being in an authentic, intimate relationship with your Soul Companion, and making new agreements with yourself based on the elemental truths that reside within you. Become the free soul that you are and your calling will resonate with the free soul who is your Soul Companion and together you will continue the journey of self-realization.

BELIEF OR TRUTH?

You are now ready to prepare a list of beliefs that have been governing your life. Beliefs are thought patterns and feelings we learned from our parents, our family of origin, and our society, usually involving dualities – right/wrong, good/bad, strong/weak, to name a few. Beliefs need to be proven in some outer way – defended, fought for, died for, or in the extreme, killed for. Beliefs inevitably clash with other beliefs, one needing to become the supreme belief or only belief. By looking at our beliefs, we can ferret out the unconscious agreements that govern our thoughts, words and actions, even though they may not truly serve us any longer. Beliefs are based on fear, hurt, guilt and assumption, and when looked upon with the light of spiritual consciousness, they evaporate into thin air. This is why they are called illusions. Usually our beliefs camouflage a truth – hiding it in plain sight – entangling and confusing the truth with illusions and lies that are bound to a certain place and time. When sharing this teaching about beliefs, Rockingbear would state, "I have never met a belief of mine that didn't turn out to be a lie."

Below are some of the beliefs that I identified during my Calling Ceremony that needed to be examined. Making this list and discovering the truths obscured behind the beliefs, was some of the most important work I did to be ready for my Soul Companion. Obviously, my list now would be different and hopefully smaller! The identification of personal beliefs is an ongoing practice on my spiritual journey.

You'll see that they are written as absolutes even though we don't operate from a singular belief at full strength. Our beliefs are usually mixed and watered down by other beliefs and some truth thrown in for good measure. It doesn't mean that we always feel this way or operate this way. When we say "part of me feels this way and part of me feels this other way," we are, in fact, identifying that we are operating from two different beliefs or a belief and a truth which are jockeying for control. In order to own the belief so that it can be untangled from the truth that it has been hiding, it's helpful to name it as an absolute as I have done here. Your task is to ferret out the beliefs that no longer serve you – about your body, sexual energy, relationships, love, personal power, money – just to name a few areas to get you started. Once you tune in to a few beliefs, the floodgates will open and pour out onto your paper.

- *I'm not good enough (as a mother, daughter, sister, friend, student, teacher. . .).*

- *Life isn't fair and justice is rarely served.*

- *Life is hard and too complex to navigate.*

- *It's better to be strong and invincible than show weakness of any kind.*

- *It's okay to be passive aggressive with loved ones and friends.*

- *If my partner loves me there must be something wrong with him.*

- *I am basically unlovable.*

- *Confrontation is scary and bad.*

- *It's easier to be nice than honest.*

- *Being labelled incompetent is a fate worse than death.*

- *I'm the sort who starts projects but never finishes them.*

- *Being vulnerable is asking to be taken advantage of.*

- *My point of view is better than yours.*

- *It's easier to walk away than participate in a discussion with opposing viewpoints.*

- *Most relationships are dysfunctional and doomed to failure.*

- *It's not okay to cry or get emotional in front of anyone.*

- *It's okay to rationalize others' inappropriate behavior toward me in order to appear understanding of their human frailties.*

- *I don't need to take advice from anyone because it's better to figure it out on my own.*

- *It's too scary to sing in front of other people.*

- *I am not worthy or equal to others.*

- *I have to become belligerent in order to stand in my power.*

- *Maintaining a strong front is better than showing insecurity and doubt.*

- *It's hard to set boundaries with friends and loved ones.*

- *Being respectful means feeling and being subservient.*

- *It's okay to be cynical and impatient to cover up anxieties.*

- *My body isn't attractive enough - hips are too wide and seems to always have 20 extra pounds.*

- *There is something wrong with people who have a lot of money.*

- *There's nothing I can say or do when someone hurts my feelings except stop being in relationship with them.*

- *It's better to put off hard conversations or tough talks because often the problem resolves itself.*

- *It's okay to be violent with myself as long as I'm not violent with others.*

TRUTH OR BELIEF?

Truths are intrinsic within us – a sense of what is just and true for us that resides in our soul connection to all the beings in the Web of Life. Truths just are. They don't have to be proven, debated, or defended. They exist in their own right. Truths co-exist with other truths, even when they are different. This is the energy of "live and let live." Our personal truths become clearer as we live through the lessons in our life. As we move into elderhood, our wisdom is based on the truths that have been revealed to us. They are not absolute truths to anyone but us, which is why we don't need to debate, argue or be missionaries to bring our truth to others. We simply need to "be our truth" so others can see the example of our actions. If it resonates with their inner truth, then we have an opportunity to share more about it, to be the teacher or master.

With 7 billion people on the planet, we need 7 billion religions, spiritual paths or traditions. In this way, each person takes responsibility for their own quest, their own journey, their own truths. We are here to learn from each other, not to be fearful of each other. That's why we are here in a physical body – to learn from all our interactions. This is Mountain Lion medicine – being a wayshower, an example, a leader without followers. Living our truths so others can see how they might do it. I have learned the most from teachers who share their truths in the form of stories and personal experience. That way I can take what I need and leave the rest. No sermons or lectures. We learn best when there is laughter, personal story and archetypal role models. Your work in the Calling Ceremony is to uncover your truths and no one else's – not your parents', siblings', childrens', friends', or other loved ones. What are your truths?

Here are the most meaningful truths that I have identified for myself while on my spiritual journey thus far. Each of these truths make sense to me because of my experiences, so they may not resonate with you at all. I've included this list simply as an example of the inner sorting work I have done and continue to do in order to winnow my beliefs from my truths. Just because I have identified an inner, governing truth, it doesn't mean that I can hold it and live it completely in my life yet. This is the ever-evolving spiral of personal growth, of enlightenment. I have found that beliefs usually number in the hundreds while truths can be counted with just our ten fingers. Your task is to make your own list.

- *Everything is perfect (right or fundamentally okay) … all of the time.*

- *I am an infinite Being of Light, evolving in a never-ending spiral of growth.*

- *There is truly enough of everything in the world for everyone.*

- *No one is special or important, but what we have each come to do and share is special and important.*

- *Everything is energy which cannot be created nor destroyed, it simply changes shape and form.*

- *Time is only present on the physical plane.*

- *As spiritual beings, we travel energetically at the speed of thought.*

- *Whatever I give attention to in my life determines my frequency and direction.*

- *The power of the spoken word sets energy in motion.*

- *Gratitude, kindness, forgiveness and acknowledgment are the most powerful transformational actions I can take to reach enlightenment.*

South Direction

HEALING, LAUGHTER, AND EMBRACING OUR TRUE NATURE

───────○────────────○───────

"All you SpiritKeepers of the South, Come, Look this way!

We give gratitude for the medicine plants
that keep us strong in body and mind.

Thank you, Coyote and Rabbit – you tricksters – who remind
us to laugh at ourselves, to not take our ego so seriously, and
for the balance of irreverence with sacredness.

Thank you, Porcupine, for your gifts of innocence,
trust and faith,
in ourselves and in every being of the Planetary Family.

So grateful for you, Stone People, who
carry the library of creation.

Thank you for our physical fitness
and each body's expression of the Divine."
Wah Doh

THE SPIRAL OF SPIRITUAL GROWTH

If we still have inner healing and transformational work to do in our relationships with our parents (and I haven't met anyone who doesn't!) we will (unconsciously) choose a partner who is similar to one of them so that we can continue learning the lessons we signed up to learn. My first marriage was a good example of that. My husband had many of the same qualities as my father. By being in relationship with my husband, I was able to better understand my relationship with my father once I realized I was repeating several patterns. It's the same work, just a different person because this work is not about changing the ones we are in relationship with but rather about changing ourselves. Realizing that, we can be in relationship with our loved ones in a different way, a way that is healing and empowering. Many of my mother's qualities that used to make me crazy are the very ones that my Soul Companion carries. They still make me crazy! But not as much – I'm getting better. Because my companion and I have a deep soul/heart connection, I am able to look at the wounds and hurts I have carried and release the pain and beliefs attached to the wounds. And that's how we learn and grow.

Spiritually, we learn and grow by moving in a spiral. Just as Earth and the other planets spiral around the Sun in their cosmic dance, so too do we spiral around the central themes of our lives. We don't evolve in a linear fashion. The spiral is a never-ending circle, with no beginning and no end, bringing us back around at different points in our lives to work with the same core issues and themes. People will come to me seeking help, despondent that the same patterns, fears, and blockages that they thought were healed are back in their lives. They think they are doing something wrong when the issue rears its ugly head again. But this is the way we continue learning and growing. We don't master an issue and then never have it in our life again. We become more skillful at handling it on finer and finer levels until we are ready to teach it. That is the final stage of learning anything – teaching it, again and again.

The issues we have come to learn about don't just magically go away because we have gained some insight into them. No, they stick around so we can experience them in different settings, seasons, places and people – from a different level of the spiral. This is the way we gain wisdom. This is how we evolve. You'll know you are getting ready to go around the spiral again when you come to a beautiful place in your self-discovery. You feel empowered, wise, filled with personal power. Everything is easy, challenges are met with grace and clarity. Enjoy this state of being!! Bask on this plateau! When we have mastered all the lessons in a current state of consciousness or "playpen," our consciousness expands, and then we realize that there are deeper mysteries we do not fully comprehend and the exploring, falling down and getting back up, looking into scary dark corners, begins again. But it's a bigger state of consciousness now – a bigger playpen. We are ever expanding, just like the Universe.

We couldn't stop evolving if we tried, but we can slow it down by falling asleep, numbing ourselves with addictions and distractions to such a point that we are not really living at all. We're breathing, but that's about it, simply going through the motions. We have all experienced this state of the "walking dead" (it's not just for Sci-Fi movies!), most often after we have been emotionally hurt or death has touched us through the loss of a loved one, but it can also come about through intense domestication. When our heart is disengaged from our interactions with ourselves and others, we become a caricature of the real self – like a talking doll or manikin.

From this level of "being asleep at the wheel," we invite someone or something else to drive our life which isn't fulfilling on the soul level.

By being awake, alert, and conscious in our lives, we can move through our learning lessons more deeply and, eventually, with less pain. Remember, the teaching about paying attention? When we are paying attention, we walk more intentionally through our days, willing to engage with the feelings and emotions being generated, with the choices in front of us, and with the consequences that come about through those choices. Paying attention is being conscious about what we are learning from our life experiences, so that we don't have to keep learning the same lessons over and over again. Isn't that the definition of insanity, "Doing the same thing again and again and expecting different results because we are unconscious of what our actions are causing?" Every spiritual tradition talks about the act of "waking up" to our true selves. And once awake, the world is a much different place – one where we acknowledge how powerful we truly are and act accordingly in creating the beauty, love, harmony and peace we so desperately desire for ourselves and the world.

We can then see the big picture with clarity and understanding. This big picture transcends what we call everyday reality – the illusion of being tied to one place and time – whereas our true reality resides beyond the limitations of space and time. As a spiritual being we continue to learn and grow without end which is extremely difficult for our left brain to comprehend. We are infinite and with this awareness of infinity, we become aware of our connection to all of life – the Web of Life that is sustained by our every thought, feeling and action. We co-create reality. We can co-create a dark, dangerous and destructive reality or we can co-create a beautiful, light, and creative reality. Or anywhere in between these two polarities. It takes an awareness of choice, a conscious desire to live in accord with the highest vibrations we can conceive of in any given moment. Like the Fibonacci spiral or golden spiral found throughout all of the natural world, we are naturally and continually expanding our state of consciousness into ever more enlightened levels of self-understanding and self-realization.

With this level of commitment to stay awake, we can truly heal ourselves and others as we navigate along the spiral of our spiritual growth and evolvement. It's as simple as seeing another person as a reflection of ourselves, as knowing that all beings experience pain, confusion and loneliness, and all beings respond favorably to comfort, kindness and understanding. We aren't here to fix ourselves or others, as no one is truly broken. All healing of the mind, emotions and body is possible when we are awake to our spiritual essence. How we live our life can be a healing to everyone we come in contact with even if we don't know it at the time. We are all healers. If you can't own that label yet, please know that you have the capacity to be a healer – everyone does. We are healing ourselves and others all the time – a twinkle in the eye, a smile that comes from the heart, a gesture of understanding, a look of respect, a gentle touch on an elder's shoulder, a willingness to listen, a gracious "thank you." All these simple acts become a part of how we impact the world on a daily basis in an unconditional way, without expectation of anything in return. Healing occurs because it is a natural part of our spiritual journey as a soul who is here to learn and grow and to love ourselves and others to the best of our ability in each moment, in each breath, in each heartbeat.

HEALING VS CURING

A wonderful example of commitment to our spiritual evolvement by requesting healing rather than being cured was lived by a woman I knew in Houston, Texas. Annabelle had danced with breast cancer for several years. When I met her, it had been in remission and then the cancer showed up again. This time around, she was actively on her spiritual journey. Now her request to Spirit was not just for the physical removal of the cancerous cells from her body; her request included a complete healing of her spiritual being, to bring back into harmony and clarity whatever was out of balance within herself. If this included being physically cured of the cancer, wonderful, but if it didn't, that was great too. She chose not to limit the healing by thinking it only had to do with her physical body. Annabelle wanted to experience healing on a soul level, and she had decided that whether that led to the cancer being "cured" and her living more years upon the Earth, or whether it meant going through the illness and her body dying, she was fully committed to actively participating in her healing journey without controlling the outcome.

Through that conscious choice for healing, she was a tremendous influence on a large number of people in her life. She wrote her own obituary as she was nearing the end of her physical life. It was filled with such joy, trust, reverence and completeness that simply by reading it, many people were healed of their fear of death. Annabelle manifested a deep commitment to healing herself in every aspect of her being – physical, emotional and spiritual. This is the level of commitment needed to live life as a Sacred Human Being. When we call for a sacred, heart-connected, truly loving, authentic relationship with a Soul Companion from this level of spiritual understanding and commitment, the relationship can and will heal you in ways you never dreamed possible. We become the one who heals and the one who is healed simultaneously.

True Nature of Violence

We often think of violence as something that leaves physical marks or wounds, even maiming or killing, but it encompasses much more than that. When we think badly of someone, we are being violent. When we think badly of ourselves, we are being violent. When we say nasty, judgmental words about ourselves, we are being violent. When we get in the way of another person's choices on how they want to live their life, we are being violent. When we expect or feel entitled to someone's love, time, energy or money, we are being violent. When we try to please others, give up our personal power, or do for everyone else but not for ourselves, we are being violent to ourselves and to others. Rockingbear talked of a certain smell and feel to this form of self-violence – toxic, putrid, and decaying. This level of violence creates a separation within from our highest, truest self. Feeling separate from ourselves and all of creation creates a chasm so that fear and the belief in lack or scarcity can take hold, coloring our perceptions. These feelings of being domesticated, isolated, controlled, fearful and powerless become normalized, making it easy to fall back asleep and accept these illusions as reality.

We talk often nowadays of the level of violence in the world. That violence is just a mirror for us to see the violence within ourselves. When the level of violence, dysfunction, disrespect and dishonoring of our Mother Earth, of the less fortunate among us, and of each other grabs our attention, it's a wake-up call to take care of the violence within ourselves. We only have the power to change ourselves and through our example be the spark for others to heal themselves. When we heal the violence within ourselves, we can then be in relationship without violence, we can create a family without violence, we can live in a community without violence, we can envision a world without violence.

On September 11, after watching the news for most of the day, I entered into a meditative state to ask my Spirit Helpers what I could do to help. I thought I might be asked to assist some of the thousands of people who were crossing over into the Spirit World, or to send energy to the rescue workers or families affected, but none of those was the task I was given. My Spirit Guides very gently said to me that if I truly wanted to help, I needed to heal the violence in my own family. The night before, my son and my Soul Companion had become embroiled in a terrific fight, each defending his own point of view with anger and hostility. I understood immediately what my Spirit Guides were telling me – to not become distracted by thinking that violence was only outside of me, that it had nothing to do with me personally. I am the only one who can take responsibility for my inner reality and how that affects every other being. The collective reality of our world is continually being co-created from all of our inner realities. That's why it's so important to stay awake and do the inner work we need to do, while, at the same time, taking the actions and non-actions to help every other being in whatever way – small or large – that is within our power to do. By paying attention, we can be part of the solutions instead of perpetuating the problems.

I no longer need a baseball bat upside the head to get my attention! I have laid down the violence against myself. I've stopped saying words to myself that I would never dream of saying to another person. Because I am a co-creator, when I say those words to myself, I am also saying them about Great Spirit. That's the way I find out if what I have said is true for me or not. If I am in the habit of saying to myself, "Robin, you numbskull! Can't you get anything right?!", then I substitute Great Spirit for myself. It sounds ridiculous when I say, "Great Spirit, you are so stupid! When are you going to stop making the same mistake over and over again? Can't you get anything right?!" That's coyote medicine – making me laugh at my own silliness. Then I can stop attacking myself that way because it's not true. Being violent against myself is a lie I learned from my parents who learned it from their parents. It's my life, so I can choose anywhere along the line to live it differently. By consciously choosing differently, I take responsibility for my life and co-create from my truths. That's why I have to look at the beliefs and the lies I learned – they get in the way of living life as a Sacred Human Being.

Teachers Come in All Shapes and Sizes

As spiritual beings, we channel our energies into a physical body so we can learn and grow. Our experiences in this world, (which I call a big school) help us continue to evolve, and, to that end, we all become teachers to one another in some form or fashion. We have the capacity to learn from every single word, act and experience. We can learn from round, soft words or hard, sharp words, from being shown a positive example or a negative one. How did your family of origin teach you? The loved ones and relatives closest to us, our friends and our co-workers are the ones we are in contact with daily and, thus, offer us the greatest opportunity for learning. When we are taught through an opposite way, it can be hurtful and traumatic with an emotional upheaval that really gets our attention. I learned from my teachers that when someone does something that upsets me, it's because I still have that same quality within myself. It may not be to the same degree, but I'm riled by their behavior because that wounded part of me is still raw and unhealed. Once I take my focus off of that other person and do my own healing, I'll still notice that behavior in others, but it won't upset me any longer. In this way, we have a continual litmus test of how we are growing and healing based on our reactions to those people closest to us. So, instead of blaming our parents, loved ones, friends and co-workers for upsetting us, we end up thanking them for helping us to learn and grow.

For example, my mother was a good one to start a project and then have trouble finishing it. Or she would talk about doing something but never take the necessary steps to actually do it. She had lots of book titles but no books. As a young adult, I found myself doing the same thing and I conveniently blamed her for passing along this bad habit. Then I learned from Rockingbear that she was actually teaching me how to finish what I started by showing me the pain and violence she experienced through the recriminations and regrets she heaped upon herself and how unfulfilled she was in certain parts of her life. When I started being grateful to her for teaching me in such a clear way how to be fulfilled, to follow through with my dreams and goals, to finish what I started or to set it down without guilt or regrets, I became more successful and happy in my life. She taught me well. She taught me through her actions and non-actions. I learned how to better live my life by seeing what didn't work for her. I have expressed my thanks to her many times even though I learned this after she passed into the Spirit World. Our loved ones are teaching us in this wonderful way. Opposites sure get our attention and are actually part of the contract we have with our loved ones! If you blame or stay angry with your family, you can't heal that part of your life and you won't learn that nugget of wisdom. Being shown our learning lessons through opposites is just one of the ways we learn and sometimes it's the very best way – not the easiest of ways, but the best way for us. Be grateful for all your learning lessons – easy and hard and the teachers in your life who love you enough to teach you through opposites! Be very grateful!

With gratitude we can heal ourselves and when we do, that healing ripples through our physical lineage in two directions – back seven generations to the ancestors that came before us and forward seven generations to our children, grandchildren and their offspring. Because we are energetically connected to our lineage through our DNA, we simply do the healing work on ourselves to affect transformation in our families. If we focus solely on our loved ones as the ones needing to change, our inner integrity is compromised and the merry-go-round of dysfunction, confusion and dis-ease continues. When we focus on the inner work we need to do to be at peace with ourselves, to be in balance with the Cosmos, to be as healed and whole as we can be in that moment, then the spiral of spiritual growth and enlightenment is automatically generated, benefitting all who are willing to embrace the transformation – either consciously or unconsciously.

TRUST, RESPECT, INTIMACY AND EQUALITY

In the Calling Ceremony, a Soul Companion is a person in a *physical* body (my spirit guides pointed out to me that I wasn't being specific enough when I left out that important detail in my own Calling Ceremony preparation) that has a deep, heart-to-heart connection with us. That connection usually has been forged over many lifetimes through numerous trials and life experiences together. There is a level of trust, a willingness for intimacy, and a depth of honesty that is naturally stimulated by being with each other. As Soul Companions, we each have an encompassing respect for the other, delighting in our differences and rejoicing in each other's talents, strengths and abilities. There is an innate feeling of equality within the relationship regardless of each partner's livelihood, level of income, education or background.

This foundation for an intimate, authentic relationship with our Soul Companion is described beautifully in *The Thirteen Original Clan Mothers*. In the chapter called *Loves All Things, Clan Mother of the Seventh Moon Cycle*, Jamie Sams shares the Clan Mother's teachings on how a relationship with a Soul Companion unfolds naturally through trust, respect, intimacy and equality when we give it time to do so. *Loves All Things* and her partner, *Feathered Dog*, gave themselves the time and circumstances to really get to know one another, to listen and learn from each other, to observe and make note of the strengths and qualities that inspired and invoked their admiration, and they shared their inner truths and selves with one another – all before becoming sexually intimate! This was certainly different from the way I had operated in relationships. I had always wanted to make sure a prospective partner was sexually compatible. Then, and only then, was I willing to invest my time to see if there was a solid connection.

I remember the first time I read *Loves All Things* – the story seemed like a fairy tale, something wonderful but not real, since relationships hadn't been that way in my experience. *Loves All Things* fascinated me but I couldn't take it all in. Each year in the seventh moon cycle, what we call July, I would read it again. Finally, after years and years, I began seeing how I could actually live the teachings of *Loves All Things* and how I could be in an intimate, authentic relationship with another who was as healed, balanced, compassionate and loving as Feathered Dog. I realized I had been going about it all backwards, putting the cart before the horse. Giving myself time to get to know another without the pressure of physical intimacy actually allowed the emotional intimacy to blossom. That was the first step in my Calling all those years ago, to realize that a relationship encompassing trust, respect, intimacy and equality was possible and I wanted it.

PAIN AND SUFFERING, HAPPINESS AND FORGIVENESS

Life doesn't have to be as hard, dangerous or violent as many of us see it right now. Ignorance of our spiritual nature and the universal laws that govern us perpetuates dysfunction within our own lives and in our society. It is a radical concept to believe "It's okay for life to be easy, joyful and filled with happiness and fulfillment," because so much of our programming from religion and societal mores teaches us otherwise. Rockingbear often shared a story that illustrates this radical concept very well. A Cherokee wise elder, Diyani Wahoo, when still a young child, was given the information held in the prophecies of her life that were received before she was born. She was told many things about her life and what she would do. Afterwards, overwhelmed by the information, she asked her Grandmother how she was to do all these things. Her Grandmother answered her, "Oh, it's simple. All you have to do is be happy. Your happiness will bring all these things onto your path." The purpose of life, as taught in the Cherokee teachings, is to be happy (an inner happiness that isn't dependent on external props). It is from this state of happiness that joy, bliss, and fulfillment flow into our lives, inspiring our creativity, abilities, healings, and teachings. I know this sounds simplistic. If I could make it more complex to satisfy the left brain I would, but it really is this simple.

Rockingbear taught that pain is a natural part of any life, but suffering is optional. We don't have to suffer because we have pain. When we simply accept the truth of what is causing the pain, the suffering disappears. I suffered with guilt for most of my life, causing much self-doubt, shyness and fear. When Rockingbear asked me point blank – what do you need to forgive yourself for? –

the tears gushed and the answer hit me like a tsunami. I needed to forgive myself for not being enough in my life – not good enough, not worthy enough, not spiritual enough, not kind enough, the list went on and on. I realized that I had been rationalizing this fear and guilt for a long time, trying to counteract those feelings by convincing myself that I was good enough, that I did do enough to help people, that I *was* enough just the way I was. My teacher then said to me, "It's okay to not be enough." Epiphany! The 2,000 watt lightbulb came on. It had never occurred to me that it was okay to not be enough. I had been striving and struggling to be enough and then punishing myself when I fell short for so long that I had forgotten how to live without that constant suffering. I simply had to accept the truth that sometimes I hadn't been enough, that sometimes I am not enough and that sometimes I will not be enough. Once I did, the suffering I experienced – the punishing thoughts, words and actions – disappeared. It's okay to not be enough. It was that simple. I still feel the pain when I perceive that I'm not enough, but my suffering isn't there. I can be more compassionate with myself and with others now.

Truths, by their very nature, are intrinsically simple – that's why the truth heals the wounds caused by illusions and lies. By accepting the truth, by going beyond our limiting thoughts and beliefs, we can forgive ourselves and forgive others. We can have gratitude even when we are grieving because grief, sorrow and pain are a part of life. Grief, sorrow and pain help us learn more about ourselves and how to live our life as a Sacred Human Being. They increase our ability to hold compassion and love. In fact, my grief has been the incubus for my most treasured dreams coming into reality. My grief in not being a mother honed my desire to have a child on my own as a single mother by choice – cutting through the confusion, doubt and circular thinking I was experiencing about how to become a mother. Because I hadn't been a mother for many lifetimes, it was a large choice for me to make – I had to be very brave. The pain of my grief from not being a mother kept washing away the energetic blood in this wound until I could see clearly what I wanted. Many of our deepest dreams and prayers are brought to life in this way – through feeling and acknowledging our grief, not running away from it or numbing ourselves as I did for many years. When we feel overwhelmed by our own grief and sorrow, or by the cosmic melancholy engendered by the disharmony still manifesting in our world today, we need to take a moment and breathe deeply. We can breathe those feelings into our hearts and then allow our hearts to expand and be filled with the illuminating rays of the sun, inviting that huge, pure energy to transform and transmute all those feelings of isolation, despair and disconnection. Then exhale harmony, peace, and love to every being in the Planetary Family. It only takes a few deep breathes with intention to shift our perspective and regain our balance. We can heal ourselves and our world in this way. Our actions and thoughts do make a difference.

There is an exceptional healing modality called Ho'oponopono – an ancient Hawaiian practice of reconciliation and forgiveness, updated for our current time and place – that helps us to be in right relations with ourselves and others. It is very simple and utterly powerful. In essence, this practice relies on four sentences to connect, rebalance and move beyond stagnating memories, strained relationships, hurts and guilt. Here is the way I practice Ho'oponopono: "I apologize for the pain and hurt I have caused. Please forgive me. Thank you. I love you." I usually do this as a solo practice in a meditative state where I visualize the person with whom I'm desiring to be in right relations. With this method, I have to be willing to make changes in my thoughts, words and actions;

otherwise, I'm apologizing for the same things over and over, without taking responsibility to do better. It is a way to humble myself and wake up my compassion.

Ho'oponopono can be an effective, general practice as well. I often offer a blanket apology to every being in the universe during the World Clearing in the Wednesday Healing Circle. Here, I'm not being specific about what I'm apologizing for as it will be beyond my conscious knowledge. It is a multi-layered apology, encompassing lifetimes of experiences and all the ripples cast by my actions, past, present and future, that have had harmful effects. By apologizing, I am taking responsibility for the pain and hurt I have caused, the ignorance and the arrogance I have perpetrated and then asking for forgiveness. I say thank you in acknowledgment that I have been heard, not necessarily forgiven, and then share my love.

What makes this such a revolutionary practice is that it is used when others have perpetuated the harm or pain – directly or indirectly – to us individually or to the collective. We turn it around and apologize to them. From this ancient teaching, if others are hurting us, then we have to take responsibility, on a soul level, for that as well. This is not condoning their behavior or thinking that we caused an individual act of pain or hurt. Taking responsibility as one of the co-creators or architects of our collective state of consciousness does not equate with causing how individuals choose to live their lives within the collective consciousness. Either we operate from the frequency that we are co-creators of our life or we aren't – it's not a part-time operating system. This way of looking at our life relieves the dysfunctional merry-go-round of the victim, perpetrator and rescuer roles. It's owning that all these roles are on the same frequency and by taking responsibility, without guilt or shame, for everything that manifests in our life, we hop off this merry-go-round and free ourselves from these debilitating and limiting roles. When I take responsibility for my life, I can be of service to all beings without taking on their burdens, and without negating their learning lessons as a soul. The Ho-oponopono practice is especially needed in our present day as we become more aware and educated regarding the everyday injustices and harmful actions that are impacting others, and thus ourselves, once removed. This energetic way of creating right relations through forgiveness is often the only realistic action we can take. Instead of feeling hopeless and overwhelmed, we can, in fact, participate in the healing of our world.

The practice of Ho'oponopono is a powerful way to take back our personal power, healing ourselves and others, and it makes it much easier to sincerely apologize in person when we need to do so. If it is an especially entangling situation, it may take years of doing Ho'oponopono before you are able to apologize face to face. I invite you to make Ho'oponopono a part of your inner clearing work. Because we are all energetically connected, our sincere apologies and requests to be forgiven can absolutely heal and reconcile our relationships.

I practice Ho'oponopono with my body as well – apologizing for the pain and hurt I have caused it in the sometimes thoughtless and harmful ways I treat and interact with it. The body carries great wisdom within its physical makeup, in and of its own right. With the utmost generosity, the body is totally willing to share that wisdom with us. If we have taken the time to develop a respectful relationship with our body – one where we are willing to listen to its signals rather than make demands of it, and work in partnership with it rather than see it as a soldier who must take orders without question – we can more easily receive the wisdom messages it is imparting and then take the appropriate actions that lead to increased health, well-being and spiritual evolution.

Rockingbear taught me that saying "I'm sorry" is fairly meaningless because it's such a big part of our domestication. In fact, he often joked that this was code for "I'm going to do it again and it's okay to do it again because I already said I'm sorry." He taught that it's more helpful to actually say what we mean. For instance, saying "I noticed I stepped on your toes and I'm not going to do that again" and meaning it, creates a powerful change agent, signaling our clear intention to keep improving our behavior and our ability to interact with others in a constructive way without feeling guilty about our learning lessons. I have found that when I say "I apologize for _____," I am owning more responsibility for my actions or non-actions than a quick and rote "I'm sorry." Any apology can be insincere, no matter what words we use, and only we can be certain that it is heartfelt.

Also, this would be a good time to look at how often you say "sorry" when what you really mean to say is "thank you." For example, instead of saying "sorry I'm late" (and you've probably been late with them before!), you could say, "thank you for waiting." Our gratitude is always more refreshing to the spirit than a rote statement coming from a place of insecurity. I love this teaching! This is a beautiful way of actively acknowledging another, rather than dismissing their feelings. Expressing our acknowledgment of another is always powerful. You'll be happier and so will all those in your life!

CO-CREATING WITH GREAT SPIRIT

As a spiritual being we are energy, energy that cannot be created or destroyed, just changed into different forms. We are a spiritual being who has a physical body. We're not a physical body that may have a soul or spirit somewhere inside us. As a spiritual being, we are the sum total of all the experiences we have had throughout eons of time. This lifetime is just a blink of an eye in the time-span of eternity. As a spiritual being, we are wearing a physical body so that we can experience and learn here on Planet Earth. Planet Earth is a big school where we learn about ourselves and life and grow and expand in consciousness. When we die, we simply leave our physical body, dropping our robes to return to our natural home – the Cosmos, Great Spirit. We return to our energetic state of being in the Spirit World.

All ideas, needs and wants already exist in the spirit realm. So when we make a request, we are simply stating that we wish to make manifest on the physical plane that which already exists. When we make a request, it is from an absolute state of acceptance of what already is. Until our requests manifest in the physical, we can perceive them and connect with them in the Spirit World with our innate, psychic perceptions. Without eyes we can see, without ears we can hear, without hands we can still feel and we have an inner knowing and awareness. With these innate psychic perceptions, we can discern the energetic reality of the request we are making. In this way it is absolutely real, it's just not in the physical yet.

Through our personal power of clarity and understanding we can consciously co-create with Great Spirit on how we wish to live our life, including our relationships with our loved ones, friends and family, co-workers, and neighbors. Through our requests, we can keep calling the life we wish to live as a Sacred Human Being. Through making requests, we are humbled by the magnificence of life and our connection to it. We can feel that connection in the synchronistic happenings in our lives. Being in the right place at the right time with the right people or right idea is a miracle. We can experience these miracles every day, even about the most mundane things.

When we request a parking space in front of where we are going, and one is available when we get there, it shows us that no request is too small or too large. But this is just a form of practicing so we can manifest the really big things in our life, like happiness, abundance, fulfillment, peace, harmony, love, respect, trust. If we are not manifesting the simple things in our life because they are trivial or not important enough, then when we need to co-create something big, like healing an illness or being in right relationship with a loved one, it will feel too difficult, overwhelming or impossible. We will be out of shape if we haven't been flexing our manifestation muscles. The spiritual fitness needed to manifest our heart's desires is not automatically maintained without attention on our part. Our spiritual fitness is no different than our physical fitness. It would be like someone expecting to run a marathon without training every day, thinking they don't want to use up their strength and endurance. It's the same for us when we think we can't ask for something small or inconsequential in our life because we don't want to use up our allotment of wishes to be granted. We don't just get 3 wishes in our lifetime, like in a fairytale. We have unlimited wishes! It doesn't matter that we've made one hundred requests this month. There is no tally. What matters is that a request has been made! Once that happens, it sets in motion all the forces in the Universe to answer that request - simply because we are loved, not because we earned it. This is unconditional love. This is the unconditional acceptance of who we are – co-creators with Great Spirit. Yes, it's vital that these requests from our soul are expressed, no matter how small, whimsical or outlandish they appear to others.

I'm reminded of a story about a young girl in a small village who was ecstatic because a circus was coming to town and she yearned to ride an elephant. Her excitement built with each passing day and she could talk or think of nothing else as her whole being wanted to experience an elephant. The day before the big event, word was sent that the circus was rerouting and wouldn't be stopping in their village. Upon hearing the news, the girl fell ill with a high temperature and couldn't eat. She became weaker and closer to death as the days went by. In desperation, her father left the village to try to find the circus and persuade them to come to his village. He didn't return with the whole circus, but he had persuaded the circus owner to allow the elephant and its handler to visit his daughter. When the elephant touched the girl with its trunk, she opened her eyes and grew stronger over the days that the elephant was with her. She recovered fully, even riding the elephant and remaining in good health after the elephant rejoined the circus. We can't fully comprehend with our left brains how riding an elephant can heal a little girl, but when her soul request was honored, her great joy and happiness brought her back into balance within herself.

It's difficult to co-create our lives when the ego is in charge. The ego is the part of us that says we're not good enough or don't deserve it, that we're not worthy enough to have what we desire, or, on the other hand, that we've worked hard, done all the "right" things, we're a good girl or boy, so we are entitled and should be rewarded. The ego makes comparisons, judgments and delineations because to have an identity it needs to compete, compare, label and categorize. But having enough gold stars stuck on a report card doesn't guarantee our prayers will be answered. Simple requests that are clear and straightforward with no strings attached are what get answered. If you have been making a request and it hasn't manifested, look at how you are making that request. Are you telling Great Spirit how your request has to show up in your life? Are you limiting co-creation by thinking you and you alone are doing all of it? Are you giving away your power thinking that you'll receive what you have asked for only if it is Great Spirit's will? It takes us both since we are co-creators with Great Spirit. When we are precise but not limiting in our requests, we will surely receive them. We might sail right by it because it may look different from the way we thought it should look. I have never had the answer to a request look exactly the way I thought it would look. Rather, it has always been better – more than what I asked for but not always in the package I was expecting. That's because I'm co-creating. I'm not in complete control.

When I make my request by stating my gratitude as if I already have it, I leave room for Spirit to work with that request. My teacher's sister always adds to her prayers "or its equivalent or something better than what I have asked." She leaves room for something even better than what she can conceive of at that time. And I add to the end of each of my requests that I am grateful that it comes to me with grace and ease. I have an agreement with myself that my life can unfold with grace and ease, that it's okay to not be hurting and in pain in order to make progress on my journey.

SHANNON'S LOVE CALLING

I met White Star at an Earth Day Fair when a friend of mine suggested I ask her for an animal spirit card reading. I did and found it accurate and helpful. White Star was open, knowledgeable, and insightful. Afterwards, my friend asked me if I was interested in meeting my soul mate. She told me White Star did a "calling ceremony" to meet your soul companion. At the time, and, actually, throughout my adult life, I hadn't had much luck with relationships. A lot of that had to do with my past experiences even though I had been exploring ways to heal. Nevertheless, I decided to visit White Star at her Medicine Lodge for a "love-calling ceremony." When I told my friend I was going to proceed with the ceremony, she said, "Get ready for someone good to come into your life!"

I began the preparations for the love-calling ceremony with White Star in early May and found it interesting and intriguing, but didn't really know what would happen. We talked about what I was looking for in a Soul Companion and what I was willing to release or give-away in order to be ready for her. I had been active on a dating site for a little over a year and had not met a suitable match. A couple of weeks after starting the ceremony with White Star, I decided to go back onto the dating site and search on the West coast (I live on the East coast). I'm not really sure why – I was just curious to see what was outside my "neighborhood." My inner voice was prompting me to pay attention. I noticed an attractive woman on the site and thought we had many things in common, so I wrote her a note – nothing ventured, nothing gained! One of the last sentences on her profile, read, "don't worry about distance – I'll come to you." I thought she was literally talking to me. She, on the other hand, was making a reference to a couple of hours away in her state, not cross-country. Unknown to me, two days earlier, she had done the exact same thing – looked outside her area and saw my profile. Anyway, I wrote to her and she wrote back. Then we spoke over the phone – often for hours at a time. We were drawn to one another. We both had experienced hurtful past relationships, and we knew the disadvantages of long distance relationships, but it all seemed to flow together for us to meet. She was in a transitional time in her career, having recently retired and had some time to travel so she did come to me. That was many, many months ago. We've spent long periods of time together and are very happy in each other's company. Our dogs get along too which was just as important to us! We are discerning where we want to live, taking into account career opportunities for me and life opportunities for her. The soul connection we feel between us has definitely created a foundation which is allowing us to go forward without fear.

What is different in this relationship? We both meet one another's values and needs on many levels – of course physical, but there is a significant resonance among our emotional and spiritual beings. We are both highly metaphysical and spiritual which we hadn't found in previous partners and we are both open to talking about what's on our minds, willing to give and receive emotional support. I never did sit with the Fire as part of my Calling Ceremony because my Soul Companion came into my life before I could do so. My love and I each requested the Soul Retrieval Ceremony and the healing we experienced has made a huge difference in how we relate to ourselves and one another. We highly recommend it. We have received many blessings and a heightened awareness of ourselves by working with White Star.

Above Direction

DREAMING OUR LIVES INTO BEING

"All you SpiritKeepers Above, Come, Look this Way!

We give gratitude to you, Starry Medicine Bowl,
for the campfires of our ancestors lighting the dark sky.

Thank you, Sister Sun and Brother Moon,
you Cloud and Rain Beings, for our lives and keeping us
company on our Earth Walks.

Thank you, Dreamtime, for that ability to travel
in our spirit bodies to experience our true natures
so we don't forget who we are.

Many gratitudes to Swan, Dolphin, Lizard and Dragonfly –
you beautiful guardians and messengers of the Dreamtime."
Wah Doh

Spiritual Guidance

Did you know you have a team of spirit guides or guardian angels whose purpose is to assist you in your life? We all have Spirit Helpers, Spiritual Guidance, Guardian Angels or our team of Higher Help – whatever you wish to call it – that is available to us 24/7. As a spiritual being, we naturally have a crystal clear communication with these more evolved souls which operated freely with us when we were younger. These guides or angels have mastered the lessons in this school we call Earth and their task now is to help us do the same. I learned at the young age of 13 that we are beings of light – pure energy that cannot be created nor destroyed. We have consciousness whether we are wearing a physical body or not. We can actively engage with this higher help through our prayers and by making requests. Paulo Coelho, in "The Alchemist," succinctly and poetically wrote, "Once you have made a request, every force in the Universe conspires to assist you!" One of those forces is your Spiritual Guidance.

I have been actively working with my angels for nearly 50 years now and I cannot imagine a life without them. They are my protectors and comforters, my advisory board and teachers. Many times they have alerted me to danger and given me instructions on the best way to protect myself. They are my confidants, reassuring me when I falter or question, helping me to stay on the main path of my life. I work with them every day and give gratitude that I am not doing this work by myself, or living my life all by myself. From this perspective, we are never alone. We always have access to crystal clear love and guidance on a very personal level. I have only to ask for their help to receive insights and clarity.

I sincerely invite you to cultivate a relationship with your Spirit Guides or Guardian Angels. Once you are spiritually cleansed and clear, begin a conversation with them by making a request or asking a question. Open yourself to receive and pay attention to the thoughts, feelings, inner knowing and pictures that enter your mind and body. By habit, you may discount or rationalize what you receive because the answers come very quickly. Trust these answers. Practice with small requests so you gain confidence. Then, when the really big stuff happens, and it usually happens when we least expect it, you'll be ready. This is a good way to stand in your power.

In the autumn of 2015, I was abroad teaching when I received a phone call telling me that my sister had been in a very bad car accident, fracturing her pelvis in 3 places and rupturing her diaphragm. I listened intently to my son as he relayed what the doctor had said – that my sister would most likely lose her spleen and possibly a kidney and an adrenal gland, while at the same time I was listening to what my angels had to say – that the surgery to re-attach her diaphragm would go well with no need to remove any other organs. I was able to stay calm and arrange my flight back because I had the inside scoop regarding the reality of the situation. I sent healing energy to my sister and niece, and repeated over and over the affirmation I was given, "Only good will come of this." My sister has a strong spirit and her physical healing went smoothly with no setbacks for the 3 weeks she was in the hospital and for the next year of rehabilitation. She too was communicating directly with her Spirit Guides to receive insight about the accident and its purpose in her life. This gave her the peace of mind she needed so she could concentrate on each step of her physical healing. Her angels were very clear with her, letting her know that she would be alright and that all the challenges facing her would ultimately be met with success.

This Calling Ceremony is all about calling upon your Spirit Guides to help you manifest what you haven't been able to manifest on your own. The more skillful you become in working with your Guardian Angels, the more easily your request will unfold in this ceremony. Any dream, vision, feeling, message, or inner knowing that comes from your Spirit Guides will be immensely helpful on your journey. You simply need to open the door to this level of communication, inviting your angels to travel with you on your journey. They are doing so anyway, but the more you consciously engage them, the more helpful they can be to you.

Spiritual Perceptions

We communicate with our team of Spiritual Guidance through the innate perceptions of intuition (clairaudience), feeling (sensory or kinetic), vision (clairvoyance) and prophecy (inner knowing). As children we perceived in these ways without thought or instruction. Most of us have had some kind of psychic or spiritual experience as a child (or later on as an adult) – knowing ahead of time about something that later came to pass, hearing our name called when no one was physically there or seeing an angel by our bedside. These can be scary experiences if our family discounted them or punished us for "telling stories," but our spiritual sensitivity is natural and necessary for a happy and fulfilling life. Everyone has all four of these spiritual perceptions but in varying degrees of openness depending on how these extrasensory perceptions were discouraged or encouraged. Through training and practice, you can unfold or open your innate psychic abilities to a deeper level, utilizing these perceptions in a more conscious way in your life. You can learn to go beyond the personal ego that filters or colors your impressions so you can truly trust that what you are picking up is correct. You can create a clear link even when emotionally invested in the outcome, fearful or experiencing panic or confusion. You can become a hollow bone, allowing your spiritual sensitivity to clearly come through when you need it most.

Our spiritual sensitivity is comprised of an innate radar system that alerts us to encroaching energies in time to respond appropriately – taking whatever actions or non-actions are needed to be safe and secure and moving through life with grace and ease. This radar system works for our physical safety and our spiritual well-being through the aura or energy field that emanates from the physical body. The aura has been photographed through Kirlian photography and can be seen through the gift of vision and sensed through the gift of feeling. When we are in a state of relaxed attention (where we want to be most of the time), the aura extends 30-50 feet or more around us, helping us to "pick up" necessary information from our environment – physically and energetically. The aura is sometimes called a buffer zone, energy field or a bubble of white light. When we are tired, ill or in a state of depression or negativity, the aura contracts, and our information gathering and extrasensory awareness to our environment diminishes. That's when we are most vulnerable. We need a reliable method to consciously align and expand our aura whenever it contracts.

In Native Traditions, smudging (the act of purifying oneself or a physical space by burning a sacred herb – usually white sage, sweetgrass, cedar or copal) is used for cleansing and aligning the energy field. It is the medicinal properties in the smoke from the plant person that purify the air and our energy fields. It clears the mind of needless chatter and helps us to come fully into the present moment. Smudging is used before entering into ceremony, sacred sites or working directly with the elementals – especially the water and fire beings. However, there are many situations in modern life where we cannot use the smoke from these sacred herbs for purification – hospitals (unless given special permission for recognized religious rites), restaurants, or courtrooms, just to name a few. Although the aura can be cleared and strengthened through the use of crystals, essential oils, sound therapy, magnets and incense, it can also be cleansed and aligned energetically, using only our own electro-magnetic energy, usually accessed through the hands. We can do this auric alignment anywhere and at any time because we always have our physical body with us! I have used many a public bathroom for this purpose – to take a moment to spiritually cleanse my energy field and expand my aura. In this way, I'm protected from any negative energies in the environment and I can more easily pick up helpful information from my Spirit Guides for my spiritual protection, attunement and purification.

ANIMAL TOTEMS

When Dragonfly caught my attention in Houston all those years ago, she led me to the *Medicine Cards*. This book and card set was my first introduction to the animal totems native to Turtle Island (the continent of North America), the medicine they carry and the skills, talents and gifts they have to offer us two-leggeds. I immediately felt a kinship with these teachings. As a girl, I had little interest in playing with dolls, but stuffed animals were another story! I had a room full of every creature imaginable, along with a real calico cat named Pumpkin. She was my best friend and heard all my tales of woe and misery while growing up, offering her furry body for me to bury my tears and calming me with her purrs. The native teachings of the animal totems resonated with me, and I gobbled up the information. Using the clear instructions given in the book, I pulled an animal totem card for each of the 7 directions. I was awed and amazed at the totems that showed up for me. The medicine they carried fit me so well, and where they were positioned on each direction made perfect sense and still does. Today I still work with those 7 totems plus others that have shown up along the way.

Whether you pull your animal totems through the *Medicine Cards* or become aware of a totem through dreams, journeying, or visions, I urge you to invite these teachers into your life. You may have been aware of an animal playmate or familiar when you were younger or simply experienced such an affinity for a certain animal that you felt like it was part of your family. It is! It's part of your spiritual guidance family. It may be a four-legged, a creepy-crawler, a winged one, or a finned one, but whatever form your totem inhabits, it holds the knowledge and wisdom that will be extremely helpful in understanding your own medicine, talents and skills.

To begin a working relationship with an animal totem, I suggest formally introducing yourself and requesting that it work with you – you can do this through a dreamtime journey or directly with the totem if present in the physical. Enter into a dialogue to discuss how you each desire to work with the other. You do this through the Language of Love which speaks heart to heart and soul to soul, transcending any language or communication barriers you may have believed exist between human and animal. On an ongoing basis, when you feel its presence close around you or see one of its kind in the wild, ask "Do you have a message for me?" Be still and listen. The answer will come almost immediately.

One day I was walking in the neighborhood and spied a red-tailed hawk sitting on a brick wall across the street from me. I stopped in my tracks and we looked at each other for quite a while. I opened myself up, checking in with my Orenda and from that place of stillness, greeted Hawk. We were still looking into each other's eyes while we were communing. I asked him if he had a message for me and he answered right away, "Pay attention – there is a gift coming your way!" When I asked for details, he looked away and then took flight. Several weeks later, I was returning from an errand on Mother's Day and there at the entrance to the next neighborhood was the red-tailed hawk – dead – struck by a car while feeding on road carrion. I knelt beside him, saying prayers of gratitude for his life. I heard him again in my mind – "I am your gift – take what you need for the Lodge." So with great reverence and an open heart, I took him home with me. His wings now help us in ceremony when

*smudging and his spirit medicine – **to trust the messages we
receive** – stays strong in the Lodge.*

I routinely ask my animal totems for help – sometimes
individually but most often together as a unit – with physical
tasks, mental clarity, assistance in my healing work, or direction
in my personal life. I pull an animal totem card every day to
give me a heads up about the energies needed, reaffirming that
a particular medicine will be especially helpful that day. At
the beginning of each year, I pull an animal totem card for that
year and for each upcoming month. I add in a sacred path card
along with receiving an intuitive key word through the gift of
clairaudience, to end up with three strands of information for the
year and for each month called a "Braid". These Braids help me
to understand the energetic container of possibilities available to
me personally.

*When I was pregnant with my son, my water broke on New
Year's Eve, but the next day I still pulled my cards and received
my key word for the upcoming year. I would walk through a
contraction, then pull a card, walk some more, pull a card, until
I had completed the roster for my year. My intuitive key word for
1993 was Joy. I pulled Hummingbird for my year's totem whose
medicine word is Joy (double Joy – lucky me!), and my sacred path
card was Sacred Space whose main teaching is about Respect. All
this information helped me to stay present with joy and hold sacred
space in each moment during the birth (I birthed at home with a
certified nurse midwife) and during that first year of life with my
son. Knowing key information ahead of time works with the gift of*

prophecy and helps me to be more intentional and conscious in my life. Plus, it's just plain fun!

When my son was around 3 months old, I was with a friend who was also a new mother, and we were pulling card spreads for ourselves. We had all the animal totem cards on the floor between us in a big cloud. My son was next to me on his stomach, wriggling and moving his arms. He lifted his head a bit and, quick as a wink, his elbow shot out, snagged a card, and deposited it under his torso. My friend and I looked at each other in shock – how was he able to do that? – and then with dawning realization that whatever card he pulled would be a very important totem for him. We gently removed the card – it was Bear. Now, this was significant because his middle name is Bear, and, at the time, I was doubting whether I had named him correctly. He was letting me know that this was exactly his main totem and his name was true. What a relief!

I am so very grateful for the many beautiful and uplifting personal experiences I have had with the creature beings over the years – a pod of male dolphins playfully zooming around at sunset in a marina on my birthday (dolphin was my totem for that year), a hummingbird showing up during my Vision Quest to confirm that my parents (both in the Spirit World) are fully available and connected to me, a Monarch butterfly alighting on me while sailing off the coast of Maine to signal that I had, in fact, transformed from chrysalis (my keyword for the trip) to butterfly in my feminine journey, and a live sea star (starfish) arriving with the tide as I was passing by on my beach walk just to say hello (this happened a few weeks before the start of 2012: The Year of Artful Communication with the Divine with Sea Star as our collective totem), just to name a few. I know you too have had meaningful personal encounters with the winged ones, finned ones, creepy crawlers and four-leggeds. These experiences show us that we are not alone on our journeys and have physical help along the way in the form of companions, teachers, comforters, messengers and healers.

The next time you encounter a creature being, center yourself and ask them, "Do you have a message for me?" Listen with your heart and the answer will come crystal clear and immediately. Trust the message!

DREAMING

The Iroquois call the dream world the "Real World." Reality resides in this intangible, invisible world beyond time and space (sometimes referred to as the "Fifth Dimension") and is always available to us. This "Real World" holds all the energies of creation, and, through our thoughts, words and actions, we are continually dreaming reality into physical beingness. We create our own reality all the time, so if we don't like our reality – either personally or collectively – we can shift our thoughts, words and actions to create something better. When we are dissatisfied, it's easy to say we want something different, but when we do the inner work needed to shift our beliefs and to dream from our truest self, then we can create something better. It's time for all of us to become conscious, intentional co-creators for the highest expression of Divine Love here on Earth. Dreaming is our natural state of being, whether we are asleep or awake. Dreaming utilizes all our gifts, talents and abilities – we essentially COME ALIVE when we are dreaming – igniting and feeding the Invisible Flame of Manifestation with our personal hope and soul desire. With the reawakening of this innate ability and practice, we become more skillful at lucid dreaming, active dreaming and intentional manifestation through daydreaming. When we embrace our personal power as co-creators – no longer willing to blame others and the past for our present reality – we move into the vibration of creation, reaching into the Fifth Dimension to birth our soul's desires.

One of the ways we can do this in community is through an all-night ceremony of dreaming, healing and reconnecting to our Truest Self. I highly recommend dreaming with other dreamers, along with the Clan Mothers and the Dreamtime Guardians and

Messengers – Dolphin, Lizard, Swan and Dragonfly. In this way we can touch, taste, smell, feel and see our unconscious dreams, graciously relinquishing the ego's desire to control our destiny and allowing our dreams to manifest in miraculous ways in the physical world. We are tapping into the Healing Medicine Bowl – a container that holds the unbirthed dreams, unrealized soul desires and forgotten goals until we are ready to bring them forth to be born with grace and ease. Dreaming these Medicine Dreams heals you, your family, your community and the world. Whether you can gather in a group to do this dreaming work or need to do it alone, know that there are dreamers all around the world that are doing this same work – dreaming the Fifth World of Peace into physical reality – as healed healers. Jamie Sams shares about the prophecy of the Whirling Rainbow of Peace in the *Sacred Path Cards* – information she received from her teachers, Grandmother Berta and Grandmother Cici. The Whirling Rainbow of Peace embodies the unity of all five races as one, no longer limited by the belief in separation, illuminating each person's unique talents and gifts to be used for the betterment of all of humanity.

TIME WEAVING

As spiritual beings, we are multi-dimensional with the ability to travel between past, present and future realities – realities that reside within us. We can't physically time travel yet, but we have always been able to do so energetically. Memories, daydreams, meditation, mindfulness, hypnotherapy and dream journeys are all useful ways to time travel. In the native traditions, we primarily use dream journeys (sometimes called mind journeys) induced by shamanic drumming to access this ability to travel freely between dimensions. In time weaving, we are not only time traveling but also intentionally catching hold of a loose energetic thread from a past experience and weaving it back into the fabric of our present day life. I'm sure that time weaving could be done with a future thread, but I have only experienced it with regards to healing past experiences.

As a way of healing, time weaving frees personal energies that are trapped within a past moment and brings that energy into the present. These trapped energies can be accessed through the strong emotions engendered from that experience – guilt, regret, shame, hurt or fear – that continue to haunt us in the present whenever these memories resurface. Some of these past experiences hold such an emotional intensity or negative charge that they effectively seal that bit of our energy in the time and place where they occurred, even while we physically continue moving on into a different time and place. This intense emotion becomes the energetic cord tying us to that past experience. We all have experiences from the past that, when remembered, bring on the same intense feelings as when they occurred – as if they were still happening. They are, but only on the energetic level. Like a sore tooth, we will return to them again and again, probing and exploring the memory even though it hurts to do so. This repetitive track creates a time loop which, when reinforced over a period of time, drains our mental and physical energies, like being on an emotional hamster wheel or mental merry-go-round. If this loop creates a small drain on our energy (as in a weak emotional charge), we can usually replenish ourselves rather quickly but if it is a larger drain (a stronger emotional charge), it can impede our forward momentum or incapacitate us altogether.

Those who have experienced trauma, abuse, serious accidents and violence, whether as a soldier in active engagements or as a civilian in everyday life, have a higher propensity to experience these large energy drains. Currently, we label this energetic reality *post-traumatic stress disorder* or PTSD. Approximately 70% of adults in the U.S. have experienced an intense level of trauma in their life, and of those, 1 in 5 go on to develop PTSD, which is about 25 million people. The percentages relating to the likelihood of developing PTSD increase as we age, women are twice as likely to develop PTSD as men, and the effects can sometimes develop many months after the traumatic event. These highly charged memories or "flashbacks" can lead to insomnia or interrupted sleep patterns, and are brought on by certain associated sounds, sights and smells which severely impact our mental/emotional health.

Time weaving is a critical healing way that transforms the past emotional charge by bringing it into the present where it can be integrated into a different, present reality. Remember, we are the sum total of every experience we have had throughout eons of time. All of these experiences – positive and negative and taken as a whole – inform who we are, how we respond to life, and impact the forward momentum of our spiritual growth.

Rockingbear introduced me to time weaving as a way of self-clearing stuck energy and bringing more life force into the present. It's not difficult to do and is well worth the time and energy involved. Time weaving is a beautiful adjunct to the Soul Retrieval Ceremony where pieces of the soul that have broken off due to trauma and violence are retrieved and returned to a person (the Soul Retrieval Ceremony is described more fully in the North Direction).

Time weaving is most effective when an emotionally charged memory surfaces spontaneously. When it does, immediately go into an introspective, calm space with deep breathing (you may have to excuse yourself and go somewhere private to do this work). When ready, in your mind's eye, the you now, of today, simply and energetically touches the past you in that experience. This intentional touch – whether visualized or kinetically experienced – creates a bridge, allowing for the transfer of energy from past to present. When that energy is deposited into the present, your body may experience a tingling sensation or a small shaking, not unlike a mild electrical shock. It doesn't hurt and actually feels pretty good! This is the body's way of dispersing the additional returning energy into its full energy system. You can do this again and again, reclaiming stuck energies moment by moment. As you drain the past charge, the mind no longer feels compelled to revisit the experience and it becomes a normal memory, remembered occasionally but not dwelt upon or obsessed over any longer. With this increase in personal energy and power, you are more fully in the present – alive, joyful, positive, directed and relaxed.

To experiment and practice, you can independently recall a situation from your past that you often think of and that has an emotional charge connected to guilt, shame, remorse, fear or any other strong emotion. Once you have recalled it, go through the steps above by energetically touching your old self to release the energy into the present. Sometimes when I'm talking with someone, my mind will take me to a memory and I'll time weave that strand of energy back into my present along with the accompanying little body shake or wiggle. I'll be asked if I'm cold and I just smile and say no, I'm fine. It takes just a nano second to do the time weaving once you become adept. I encourage you to give time weaving a place in your personal healing practice.

I experienced a major time weaving event in the summer of 2004 when my son and I took in the just-released movie Harry Potter and the Prisoner of Askaban. My partner, son and I were overnighting in Hendersonville, North Carolina, in order to drop off my son at the Eagle's Nest Camp in Brevard early the next morning when my son realized that the movie had opened that day and he wouldn't be able to see it for the 3 weeks he was away at camp. It was already late, and my partner didn't want to go with us, but I agreed to take my son to the late showing as it was a fun, last thing to do together before camp started. We thoroughly enjoyed the movie and I especially liked the time traveling that Hermione learned which came in very handy at the end of the movie.

It was shortly after midnight when we left the theatre and entered the parking lot. At that moment, it seemed as if I had walked into a wall of energy. It jolted me and I began crying. My son walked beside me to the car, all the while I was crying. I just sat in the car, unable to drive. My 11-year old son finally said in a soft voice, "Um, Mom, I really didn't find the movie all that sad." With that, the spell was broken and I began to calm down. When I could talk, I shared with him what had just happened.

I used to go to this same theatre in Hendersonville when he was a toddler and I was still a single mother. I would wait until he had fallen asleep and since I shared the house we lived in with my parents, they would watch over my son while I would go see a late movie by myself. It was always after midnight when the movie let out. I remembered feeling so alone and lonely on those nights, adrift and lost, despairing really, unsure if I would ever be in the love relationship I so desperately desired (this memory was from about 3 years before I experienced the calling ceremony). I had just smacked into my old self carrying all those old emotions right there in the parking lot of the movie theatre. The integration of the intense longings I held then for what I now had in the present brought about an emotional release that left me full of wonder and gratitude, warmth and quiet joy. If my son and I hadn't attended the late movie, I wouldn't have encountered my old energy pattern and I wouldn't have so quickly transferred the past emotional energy into my present life.

Below Direction

SITTING WITH THE FIRE

———◦—————————————◦———

"All you SpiritKeepers Below, Come, Look this Way!

Pacha Mama, Gaia, Mother Earth! Thank you for our Lives!

Thank you, all you Children of the Earth Blanket,
you creepy-crawlers, you winged ones, finned ones,
four-legged ones, you pollinators and
regenerators who keep us alive.

Many gratitudes for the diversity of life,
for the interconnectedness of life, to the Web of Life and the
equality of each member of the Planetary Family.

Thank you, Mother, for teaching us how to take care
of you, to honor all life forms, and to walk gently
upon you with love and respect."
Wah Doh

ARE YOU READY?

When you know you are complete with all your preparations and your medicine teacher knows you are complete, it's time to sit with the Fire. When you requested the Calling Ceremony, it began. You may think that sitting with the Fire is the most important piece of the ceremony, that only then are you actually in ceremony, but that would be an illusion. All of the preparation – winnowing the beliefs that no longer serve you from your truths, discerning who you perceive yourself to be, becoming clear about who you are calling into your life and the energetics of the relationship container you wish to sustain – all are equally as important.

Without this very thorough and deep inner work, your time with the Fire wouldn't yield the fruit you desire – to meet and connect with your Soul Companion. Your task is to become so clear, so light in your heart and mind, so grounded in your truths, so trusting in yourself and Spirit, that when you sit with the Fire, you can fully reveal yourself as a Being of Light. This entails a willingness to be the perfection you are in every moment, to absolutely open your heart to be ready to show yourself – all your power, grace, love, AND vulnerability – to your Soul Companion. Then when you sense your Soul Companion through the Fire, you will know them for who they truly are as well – another Being of Light, perfection made manifest. This soul perfection has nothing to do with being perfect. We are not here to be perfect, we are here to be love and compassion and understanding and forgiveness. You and your Soul Companion will never be perfect, but you are perfectly right for each other in order to continue your life journeys together.

Do not be concerned that your Soul Companion has not, most likely, experienced a Calling Ceremony or done the work in the same way as you have in order to be ready for this intimate, authentic relationship. They will have done what they needed to do in their own way, perhaps consciously, perhaps not. There will be equality between you, as you have both walked through the Fires in your lives to become who you are in this present moment, ready for each other as Soul Companions.

SHARING YOUR GRATITUDE TO THE FIRE

Regardless of the size of the Fire you sit before – a single candle flame or a roaring bonfire – it carries the same power and ability to transform and clear energy. This power is absolute – physically and energetically. Whenever you wish to move from one frequency to another, sit with the Fire and give away all thoughts, emotions and beliefs that no longer serve you, all that no longer resonates with the frequency you desire. The Fire is happy to assist you when you desire inner transformation because that is its nature – it is being true to its medicine – to receive what is offered and transform the contaminated thoughts, emotions and beliefs into pure, raw energy (heat and smoke) to be carried on the Winds to Great Spirit. Just as each of the elementals of Air, Water, Fire and Earth transform dead physical matter to keep the wheel of life, death and rebirth turning, so too do they transform the energies of discarded thoughts, deadened emotions and untenable beliefs, breaking them down into useable, free energy, available to everyone. Through conscious intention, ritual and ceremony, we can actively participate in the dance of life with the standing ones (trees), the plant people, the four-leggeds, the creepy-crawlers, the winged ones, the cloud people, the star beings, the water beings, the wind people, the fire beings, and all the children of the earth blanket – essentially all the beings of Mother Earth and our Planetary Family – to alchemically transform our fears, insecurities, anger and prejudices into love, compassion, harmony and respect. This is why we invoke all these beings when we begin ceremony, to invite all of them to work with us in the requested transformation. It's important to recognize that we are not doing this work alone – we have all the help we need. It's also important to give back – to feed the holy – by stating our gratitude and love, and acknowledging the help we have received.

One of the prayers that Rockingbear shared in his teachings is: *I send you my love, I send you my gratitude, and I acknowledge you.* I say this prayer to Rockingbear and all my teachers each day, and to each being I meet along my path, especially the Water Beings whom I love so well. It's essential that we speak our gratitude and love to all the beings in our life, especially our loved ones, friends, and co-workers. Don't wait. You never know if you will see them again. When we speak our gratitude so that others can hear, it is a blessing and a healing for ourselves and for the one who is receiving. This is true praise when we can share with another our gratitude for their life, their work, their way of being in the world that ripples out to eventually touch every being in the world. We also need to practice receiving gratitude and love from others. If we only give and are not open to receive then we are actually being stingy, not allowing another to give. We all have to take turns in giving and receiving if there is to be balance.

I have participated in hundreds of Fire Ceremonies over the years – each one an opportunity to shed a part of me that I had outgrown and to do so with gratitude, humility, respect and love. It's not advisable to get too cocky around the Fire! We have all been burned somewhere along the line which taught us to respect and honor the medicine that Fire carries. When I sit with the Fire, I share my gratitude to the Fire along with a pinch of tobacco, cornmeal, cedar or salt. Sometimes I use other herbs as well – whatever I feel led to share with the Fire. It could be lavender, dried flowers, acorns, pinecones, beeswax, chocolate – the possibilities are endless.

My first experience with a Fire Ceremony was in Houston, Texas, as part of a Feminine Journey class I was taking at the Jung Center. We assembled on a woman's land outside the city and each approached the Fire in turn with an offering of what we wanted to transform in our lives. In preparing for this, I discerned that my heart was closed and barricaded, protected by barbed wire. Shameful and hurtful experiences had caused enough pain that my heart had shut down to keep intimacy at bay. To create my offering to the Fire, I found some cedar hearts with holes at the top which I strung on a ribbon, wrapped them in a tangled mess along with a "no trespassing" sign written on paper. When it was my turn, I shared with the group of women what I was releasing and then gifted my offering to the Fire. It was a beautiful experience and awakened my desire to appreciate and participate in ceremonies.

The next day, I was, as usual, running late for work and was speeding along the road when I was pulled over by a traffic cop. When he approached the car, he asked forcefully, "Do you know how fast you were going?" I burst into tears – sobbing uncontrollably. In that moment, I was owning how fast I had been running away from vulnerability and intimacy. This release came on its own accord, and I couldn't stop it. The officer took pity on me and waited until I had calmed down, told me to slow down and sent me on my way. I am forever grateful to him for his help in completing the transformation and healing which I requested at the Fire. Sometimes it occurs very quickly like in this story, and other times it may take days, weeks, months or even years, but it will happen. Great Spirit is forever patient and has an excellent memory!

SITTING WITH THE FIRE

Upon the day and time appointed, you will gather your altar pieces and gifts for the Fire, dress in your finest ceremonial clothing and present yourself to the Fire. After ritual cleansing, clearing and blessing with Beautiful Water, you will sit before the Fire, within range to share gifts of tobacco, cedar and cornmeal and any other gifts you wish to share. You speak, chant or sing the gratitude you hold in your heart for your life, for the inner healing work you have undertaken and for the assistance of all the beings of the Planetary Family who have agreed to help you in calling your Beloved to sit on the other side of the Fire and make his or her presence known to you.

In this culmination of the Calling Ceremony, you share with the Fire who you perceive yourself to be and who you are calling to come into your life as your Beloved, and you ask the Fire to beckon and magnetically draw your Beloved to sit across the Fire from you. In this initial meeting you are making the energetic connections so you can more easily meet each other in the physical. Through the shamanic beat of the drum, you are carried into an altered state, which is your natural soul state. With your psychic perceptions, you may "see" an image or symbol of your Beloved, "hear" their voice or thoughts, "feel" their intentions and their individual, unique vibration or "simply know" the essence of your Soul Companion. Being introduced to one another through the illuminating power of the Fire gives you an amazing sense of connection, trust and knowingness that you will recognize each other when your paths cross in the physical world. All the doubt, insecurity, and apprehension disappears, replaced with a sense of calm, clarity and sureness that will sustain you during the final phase of making the physical connection with your Soul Companion.

With intention and clarity of purpose, you humble yourself and open your heart to receive the help requested. You sit with power and presence, becoming one with the Fire. Your imagination is activated. The portal opens between your rational mind and your heart, liberating your spirit to freely fly like the Arrow of Truth released from the Bow of Beauty. You catch a glimpse of your Beloved and they are magnificent.

LOOKING THROUGH THE FIRE

The power of the Fire aids you in getting out of your own way at this crucial time of revelation. The beauty of the Fire helps you gently move the ego aside, engaging your highest self to be transparent. Great Spirit becomes the cosmic matchmaker, transporting you from limited vision to an expanded consciousness that magnetizes and calibrates your vibration with the vibration of your Soul Companion. There is alchemical magic residing in the very nature of Fire, willing and able to carry you into the most expressive and open state of consciousness – to bare your soul, so to speak – for you to look into the Fire and see, hear, feel or sense your Beloved's presence. It is a moving, wondrous and intoxicating experience – to connect with your Soul Companion through the Fire.

Now is the time to formally introduce yourself to your Beloved – who you perceive yourself to be, where you are in your life and the journey you have undertaken. It's helpful to talk out loud, voicing the words that need to be shared from your heart. Let your Soul Companion know how grateful you are that they have heard the call and have come to the Fire to make this energetic connection. Listen as they introduce themselves to you. Once these introductions and initial sharing between the two of you are complete, you could ask them, "Do you agree to be a Soul Companion to me in the physical world so we can travel together on a path of personal growth and spiritual unfoldment with love, intimacy and authenticity?" If the answer is yes, you would also agree to the same. Please personalize the wording to fit your own individual way of seeing your path forward together. This agreement activates the frequency or resonance of the sacred union energetically being formed between the two of you. In other words, this serves as the foundation for the relationship and influences how it will continue to unfold as you journey together on this path of being in relationship with your Soul Companion.

Any other words that need to be spoken aloud to your Soul Companion and words you need to hear from your them can be exchanged at this time – these may include the places you each frequent and the activities you most often engage in, so you can physically find each other, and any other relevant information as to timing. If you like to hike and often go to a certain location, make sure you let them know. Or if you belong to a book club, dance group, or any other regular activity, be specific with days and times. In this way, you are opening your life and inviting them to become a part of it, making it easier for them to find you. Pay attention to what you are hearing from your Soul Companion about the places they will be and their activities as well so you can be in the right place at the right time to physically find one another.

JOURNEYING WITH THE DRUM

The shamanic beat of the drum attunes your brainwaves, helping you move into the Alpha state of deep relaxation and heightened visualization and then on into the Theta state – an even deeper place of relaxation, spiritual connection, insight and pure feeling experience – beyond time and space, beyond words and thoughts, into the realm of silent knowingness. Allow this dream journey to unfold naturally with your Soul Companion, dancing or moving together energetically, being your most authentic self and embracing theirs. Remember, you may see images, hear sounds and words, feel vibrations and energy or simply know what is transpiring around you as you become aware within the dream journey.

This may be a time when you are led to enter into the Turtle Council House in the Spirit World where the Thirteen Original Clan Mothers do their healing work and ceremonies for further cleansing, blessing and healing. Or you may find your Medicine Ancestors and those of your Beloved lifting you both up in celebration and acknowledgment for all the inner attunement work you each have done, the giving away of fears and limitations, and the opening of your hearts to each other. Let your spirits soar together, embracing each other and the world in your happiness.

There is no wrong way to experience a dream journey. Simply allow the drumbeat to carry you into a dream state to experience all there is for you to experience in that moment. It's okay not to see visually at first. Many people expect their dream journey to look like a movie but not everyone has the gift of vision unfolded to the degree where they can do that. You will experience the same information whether you see it, hear it, feel it or know it. And it's okay to not consciously record anything of the dream journey, although that means missing some of the fun of it. Trust that you know how to do this, relax and allow it to unfold. It is the most natural state of being – we have to work really hard and expend a huge amount of energy to stay in the ego perspective. The more you dream with the drum, the easier and fuller your experiences will be. If you don't have an experienced drummer on hand to drum for you, you may want to listen to recorded shamanic drumming.

When the drumming stops, it is your signal to wrap up your journey and come back to the present time and place. You don't have to rush back, rather you can allow your journey to conclude naturally and then return. When we journey with the drum we are outside of time, in the realm of the Fifth Dimension, and so a lot can be experienced in a fairly short amount of time. The Medicine Healer who is drumming for you will listen to the drum and know when to begin and end. Like other extrasensory experiences, it is usually helpful to keep the experience close to your heart as you absorb and digest all that it has to offer you before sharing it with others. This is entirely your discernment to make – when and with whom to share your experience.

As you prepare to take your leave from the Fire, share your gratitude once again for the assistance you received in connecting with your Soul Companion. As the ceremony draws to its natural conclusion, know that you will carry within your heart this dream journey experience of being together, keeping the Invisible Flame of Manifestation burning brightly, so you may more easily find each other in the physical realm.

Within Direction

INNER SACRED SPACE

———————○———————

"All you SpiritKeepers Within, Come, Look this Way!

Medicine Ancestors! Personal Ancestors!

*Thank you for the wise choices you made in your lifetimes
to sustain and nurture us, to pass down
the wisdom and knowledge
so we can better live our lives as Sacred Human Beings.*

*Thank you to the next seven generations, reminding us to
make wise choices with intention and respect, to
pass down the knowledge and wisdom gained, and to create
beauty and balance upon the Earth."*
Wah Doh

FEEDING THE HOLY

When we live our lives as Sacred Human Beings, following the truths and agreements that reside in our hearts, we flow with the rhythms of the universe and our Planetary Family, co-creating our dreams with Great Spirit, nourishing ourselves, each other, and the Medicine Ancestors with our gratitude, songs and prayers. This conscious expression of the Divine, or the Sacred Self that resides within, helps all other beings migrate in their lives so that they can be in the right place, at the right time, connecting with the right people in order for their dreams to be realized and manifested on the physical plane. We call this "feeding the holy." With our thoughts, words and actions in congruent alignment, we become healers to ourselves and others. Our life "grows corn." In other words, our lives are filled with joy, peace and harmony to such an extent that others benefit from our abundance.

Now is the time to stay in the vibration of deep gratitude. Remember, you are still in ceremony! By staying in your gratitude for the Soul Companion you have made contact with through the Fire, you are strengthening the cord or woven strand that is bringing you together in the physical. Sometimes you will have a sense as to when you will meet one another. When I was sitting with the Fire, I had the inner knowing my Soul Companion and I would meet each other physically within the year. I sat with the Fire in January of 2000 and we met physically that December (after making initial contact in November). Others have shared various time frames with 9 months most often being sensed. And if you don't have a sense of the timing, that's okay too – one woman felt that if she knew the timing, her left brain would over engage and it would be too much pressure. I found it helpful to know that my calling would take about a year. It kept me from growing despondent or giving up before the miracle occurred. It was taxing though, to be sure, as it was difficult to wait that amount of time!

Whatever the timing, whatever the circumstances in which you meet one another, the heart connection you share, forged in the flames of the Fire, will stay strong. Feed it with gratitude. Remember, state your gratitude in the present. It is already here. You just haven't seen it yet in the physical. "Thank you, Creator, for this beautiful Soul Companion in my life! The love and trust we share helps me so much! Life is sweet, Creator, and my heart is full of joy!" When we pray with gratitude in this way, we feed the holy – the Medicine Ancestors and all the beings of the Planetary Family – which in turn feeds us. It's a beautiful, reciprocal way of living life.

RELEASING YOUR SCENT

You have met your Soul Companion through the Fire, each giving and receiving a token to acknowledge the sacred connection you share and the agreements you have made within yourself and with each other in order to be together in an intimate, authentic relationship. You are giving voice to your gratitude to Great Spirit through prayers, song, dance and any other artistic expression to continue the magnetization of drawing your Beloved into your life and arms.

Now it's time to release your scent – the essence of who you are – into the physical realm so your Beloved can track you and find you by your scent. What is your scent? It is all of what makes you a unique human being, the sum total of all the experiences you have had throughout eons of time. It is your willingness to be heard, to be seen, and to be found. It is your way of altering the physical habits of your life so that you are exploring, stretching, and embracing all of who you are at any given moment in time and listening so you can follow the snake of your life. There is only one woman that I know who was able to meet her Soul Companion by staying at home – he knocked on her door one day with a UPS package for her!

For me, it was being open to online dating sites – taking the time to be honest and thoughtful in my profile, knowing which picture of myself to post, being up-to-date and real – and making an agreement with Spirit that I would answer all inquiries with an open heart and open mind. I released my scent in the voluminous writing I sent in response to each and every query, absolutely allowing myself to be heard and seen. I released my scent by accepting various offers to meet for lunch, coffee, or to go dancing, not prejudging how I thought the experience should go. I released my scent when I invited the man I had been talking with by phone for 3 weeks to visit me in Asheville for a face-to-face meeting, offered him a place to stay for the night and introduced him to my son, father, sister and niece that same weekend! I trusted my instincts and inner knowing and discerned what actions to take to feel safe and secure for this first physical meeting. Other people I have worked with in this ceremony have released their scents in very different ways – for one women it was making the first move with a man she had been friends with since high school, inviting him for a dinner date; for another it was joining a trendy gym that earlier she had sworn she would never join with the challenge of being herself and not competing with the other women there or judging herself; and for another it was updating her "look" and buying bright-colored clothing that she had always wanted but denied for herself.

There are countless ways to release your scent and you won't even know what it fully entails until you are at this point in your calling. You can't figure it out ahead of time – it's one of those "you'll know it when you see it" kind of things. It's not one size fits all. It will be unique and individual to your calling. As you continue to listen and pay attention to the inner promptings of your heart, you'll be led to be in the right place at the right time to connect with your Beloved. As you continue to live your life from a place of gratitude, your scent will naturally waft before you, awakening and enticing your Beloved to listen and pay attention, to better recognize you physically when you meet one another.

Meeting your Soul Companion in the Physical

The moment will come when you actually meet your Soul Companion in the physical world. The commitment to yourself, all the inner transformational work you have done, and sitting before the Fire with crystal clarity and integrity have all prepared you for this initial meeting. For many, the attraction is instantaneous, the comfort level high with mutual feelings of trust and respect that form the foundation on which to build the relationship. There is a feeling that you already know each other and have been waiting to see each other again. And for some, this initial meeting in the physical isn't what was expected or desired. Instead, it is a test of newly discovered inner truths and the ability to navigate hidden whirlpools of emotions. There follows a period of questioning and adjustment. Mine was the latter experience which, in all humbleness, I share with you now as a learning lesson, an example of an incongruence between soul knowledge and the physical reality of what our Soul Companion looks like in this present time and place, so that, hopefully, you will be more fully prepared and can adjust more quickly than I was able to if this same issue applies to you.

As you will remember, I had been spending many hours talking on the phone and emailing back and forth since I had first answered my Soul Companion's online dating inquiry. Since we lived in different cities but both in North Carolina, we knew that a physical meeting would take place, but we needed to find the right time between our schedules. Through many conversations, often late into the night, we quickly became close emotionally – sharing our personal stories, the individual paths that led us to be seeking a relationship, our hopes and desires for a loving relationship and for the future. There was a level of intimacy and trust that I found astonishing and delightful. We held many similar values and had arrived at common truths via different but ultimately similar paths. He had seen my photo with my online profile (which he recognized on a soul level) and had sent me his – a photo of him that was taken on a beach outing with family a year earlier. He had talked with my son on the phone a few times (he didn't have any children of his own, just nieces and nephews) and totally accepted my love and devotion to him. We were already feeling great trust, respect and love for each other, thrilled with our long distance romance and ready to meet.

We agreed upon a weekend where he would make the 2½ hour drive, all three of us would go for a pizza dinner, he would stay over in the guest room and then meet my father, sister and niece the following day at a family get-together. It felt right and I was ready for this next step – nervous and excited. When the day came, my son was playing with friends in front of the apartment and ran to tell me that "he" had just driven up. I did a final recheck in the mirror and then, there he was at the door, smiling shyly. He looked at me and I looked at him. I saw the look in his eyes that said I wasn't quite what he had expected and with that initial look, my heart shut down. He recovered quickly but it made for an awkward and uncomfortable physical introduction. I felt a disconnect even after all our intimate conversations. It was a surreal several moments. Inside I was dying – unable to talk about what I was feeling in that moment – judgment, criticism and that, again, I had been found "not good enough." I recovered more slowly but did regain my balance as we continued talking, deciding to keep to our schedule and see where our interactions would lead. We had a fun weekend but not the one I had hoped for, as a part of me was still holding back.

Later, we shared that each other's physical appearance had taken us by surprise, even though we had seen a few photos of each other. He was used to petite women so I was larger than the women he had been with. He appeared skinny and too fine-boned to fit with my idea of what my man should look like – beliefs I wasn't even aware I held. I didn't want to be able to beat him in arm wrestling! I could still feel the deep connection we had forged earlier and because of that soul connection, through the days and weeks afterwards, we were able to keep the door open to see whether our relationship could survive that first meeting. We talked about the beliefs that had been activated, shared concerns about sexual chemistry (my fear that I didn't feel any between us), its importance in a relationship and whether it could be discerned immediately or needed time to grow, and worked through those initial reactions of "Oh no, there must be some mistake, you couldn't possibly be my Soul Companion!" We were forced to look at the incongruence between our beliefs and the truths we felt in our hearts. Even after all the work I had done to dismantle my beliefs, the social expectations of what my Soul Companion should look like were contaminating the emerging relationship.

I was scheduled for surgery towards the end of the year and I decided that it was best to not continue the relationship, as I needed all my focus, strength and energy to prepare for the surgery and to recuperate afterwards. But my Soul Companion had a different idea. We hadn't seen each other since that first weekend when he showed up unannounced the night before my surgery. I was just on my way to do an errand when I saw him get out of his car. The sight of him made my heart leap in gladness and I realized how happy I was to see him. He helped me that evening with my final preparations for surgery and was there when I came home – bringing me food and drink as I couldn't navigate the stairs, coordinating my son's childcare arrangements and being the overall point person for my recovery. I had never been taken care of by a man and it was absolutely delicious! We talked endlessly (when I wasn't sleeping) and reaffirmed that deep heart and soul connection. From that moment on there was never any doubt in either of our minds that we were indeed Beloveds, the Soul Companions that we had searched for and wondered if we would ever find. We did. And, as an aside, my fear that we didn't have sexual chemistry was to our delight, completely erroneous.

Upon later reflection, I realized that I had tested him, although I had done it unconsciously. I was genuine and authentic in my distress, doing my best to navigate through the emotionally charged waters of my beliefs. I couldn't think my way through it, so, in essence, I surrendered to what I was feeling. But my Beloved, following his intuition and guided by his heart, gave us a second chance to meet again and surprised me in a way where I could feel and acknowledge my response to him. We both persevered, in our own way, because the soul connection was already in place, the gifts given and received in troth, through the Fire and before Great Spirit.

So take heart, even if your first meeting is a bit rocky. Know that if this other person is truly your Soul Companion and you have each done the inner work necessary to be together, then all will unfold with grace and ease by "following the snake" as intuited by your hearts. You truly can live happily ever after.

RIPPLE EFFECT OF MANIFESTATION

After I met my Soul Companion, my son and I moved to Winston-Salem from Asheville, North Carolina, to be with him. I needed to let the people of this new place know who I was – that I was a teacher and a healer and I was willing to be of service and share the teachings I had learned to the best of my ability. I began moving inward, listening to my Orenda – my still, inner voice – to begin the creation of a new spiritual community and to make my requests to Great Spirit. Each person makes their requests known on this energetic level slightly differently. For me it is drumming. This is how I make my requests, asking the winds to carry my words to all the ears that are ready to hear. As I drummed, I sang my prayers and requests, my "hello and this is what I do" and "I'm here to be of service" and "Come, come all you beautiful people who are looking for a teacher and a healer in the Native ways." I drummed often and let all the beings in the Universe know that I was available to do my healing work in this time and place. My partner would ask me when he returned from work if I had networked that day and I could answer truthfully, Yes! This is the way I know to network – first laying the energetic groundwork, then taking the actions and non-actions that present themselves.

And I listened and paid attention. I heard from several sources about a gathering place for women called Whistling Women, and so one day I went to breakfast there; I met the owner, Mary and her partner Starr, and talked about my work. Mary was excited about women drumming together and we arranged that I would be part of an upcoming street fair and offer the Clan Mother circle to interested women. Everything fell into place. I met more like-minded people through the street fair than I could have in any other way. Thirty women showed up for the first Clan Mother Circle. I had been in town for just 3 months and my work was taking off beautifully. I made a calling, set energy in motion, and then I listened and paid attention. I co-created my dream with Great Spirit who led me to Mary who helped me co-create it further. I did my 50% which was to pay attention and take the actions I needed to take. Everything else was done on the energetic level. One woman came up to me after the street fair and shared that she and her partner had been asking for a teacher in the Native ways to come to town! So I was also the answer to her calling, to her request just as she was the answer to my calling, my request. Our journey can be fun and joyful when we work with Spirit, taking responsibility for our dreams and desires and asking for assistance.

So too will you be the answer to your Soul Companion's prayers and requests, just as they are to yours. Your calling will probably not end with the meeting of your Soul Companion. Like me, you will continue to call a new life, arm in arm with your Beloved, into physical manifestation. I call this the win/win/win situation. We win, our Soul Companion wins and all those we touch in our families, our communities and in the world win because a deeper level of clarity, joy and connection has been made which strengthens the Web of Life that feeds us all.

SPIRITUAL DAILY PRACTICE

If any of the medicine teachings, tools or techniques presented herein speak to you, I ask that you take them and create a spiritual daily practice. It is through simple, repetitive intention and ritual that we shift our thoughts and emotions into the life we wish to truly live. As you will see in the daily practice I keep, it can be simple and not time consuming. It's more helpful to do 5 minutes every day, than ½ hour every month or so. In sharing my personal daily practice as it's evolved, my hope is to spark your imagination, with no desire that you copy my practice.

Each morning upon waking, I state my gratitude to Grandfather Sun and Grandmother Moon for my life. If the Earth was closer or further away from the Sun we would not have life as we know it on this planet as it would be uninhabitable due to extreme heat or cold. If the Moon was closer or further away from the Earth, we would not have the atmosphere that we rely on to breathe, as it is the gravitational field between Grandmother Moon and Mother Earth that keeps the atmosphere from floating away. In greeting them each day, I am acknowledging that there is a Divine Plan in place and I am a part of it. It is my way of affirming my connection to all of life. I spiritually cleanse myself and check in with my Spirit Helpers. I pull an Animal Totem card for the day to see what special medicine is available to me for the day's upcoming events and healing sessions. On special or ceremonial days, I greet the rising sun by singing the Cherokee Morning Song to welcome in the day. All this takes about five minutes, but the benefits last all day.

At mid-day, I stop what I'm doing and go outdoors to face the sun and say my gratitudes to the Medicine Ancestors, to the spiritual traditions that feed me, to my teachers and to my personal ancestors and loved ones. I find that this reconnection in the middle of the day keeps me on track and mindful. I start with my hands together at my third eye, sweeping my arms overhead and then folding at the waist to touch the ground with each gratitude. Again, I invest about 5 minutes to do this. I continue cleansing and smudging as needed throughout the day, depending on the work I am doing.

Then in the evening, I regroup how I walked as a Sacred Human Being that day – taking inventory regarding improvements needed and how I have become better, then doing the Ho'oponopono practice of forgiveness with friends and loved ones and with every being in the Universe and ending with more gratitudes. From here I often drift into sleep. These are some of the daily practices that sustain me. As you can see, they are not time consuming or require special places or equipment – simplicity and ease are part of my spiritual practice! I also meditate, practice yoga, journey with the drum and feed my spirit with beautiful ceremonies and healing circles. I talk with every being I meet along my way, whether animal, plant or mineral – all enrich my life.

Chances are you already have a spiritual daily practice and, if so, you can check to see if any parts of it need to be updated or changed to reflect who are in this present moment. It's okay to be playful and have fun with your daily practice to keep it alive and fresh. Listen to your Orenda for specialized instructions and innovations. Rockingbear observed that spiritual seekers often become too serious, shutting down their playful, light energy to the detriment of their health and well-being. As a Being of Light, we can embrace all of us in our daily practice.

If you don't have an established daily practice, I invite you to craft one – start simple with one ritual and then add to it as your Orenda guides you. It is in these daily practices that many of your insights will arrive, quickly and without fanfare, like old friends who drop in unannounced but always welcome. You are here to express your uniqueness as a soul for the betterment of all. You are worth the time and energy it takes to connect to Great Spirit and be replenished and renewed with joy, peace and healing energy for your health and well-being. Remember, you don't have to harm yourself or be harmed by others in order to share your gifts and talents with the world – the harm that comes from not taking care of your physical body, from consistently giving more than you are receiving, or being violent and abusive with yourself. A daily spiritual practice simply means you are staying engaged with Spirit so you can be a more intentional co-creator of the world you wish to live in every day.

Blessing

Since there is no word for goodbye in the Cherokee language, I leave you with this simple blessing:

May you and your Beloved live and love well,
sharing your talents, gifts and medicine
with the world to the best of your abilities.

May this calling of your Soul Companion
be the springboard to a deeper practice
and fuller experience of being a co-creator.

May all the beings of the Planetary Family
benefit from your healing, happiness and love.

And may you and your Beloved be fierce in
your expressions of happiness and joy.

Thank you for this opportunity to be of service to you on your spiritual journey and to share, to the best of my ability, the wisdom I have absorbed from the teachings of Will Rockingbear. These are my words. Wah Doh.

Love, Gratitude and Acknowledgement

To Will Rockingbear for accepting me as an Apprentice, helping me to heal the wounded aspects of myself, and teaching me the indigenous ceremonies and traditions you carried, all while exuding unfailing humor, integrity and wisdom. It gives me great comfort knowing you are sitting at the campfires of the Ancestors in the Starry Medicine Bowl, keeping the stories alive!

To those who sat in the Monday Night Healing Circle with Rockingbear at Earth Green Medicine Lodge through all the years, but especially to Bo Rose, Carolyn, Dawn, Mark, Ashley, Vicky, Amanda and David. Those magical nights will live forever within my heart.

To all the elders, apprentices and students who showed up at the Vision Quest Ceremonies, year after year, practicing how to better live life as a Sacred Human Being. Heartfelt gratitude to Vision Quest Chiefs Keith Thunder Bear, Steven, Rich (many thanks for the gift of the rattlesnake skin), and Flavia; to Fire Chiefs Jim, Greg (deep gratitude for your recovery of the Eagle Song), and Tim (13 thank yous for your generosity through the years); to Kitchen Chiefs Sharon Blue Otter Woman, Usha, Miriam Firebird (grateful for how you feed the ancestors), and Amy; and to Tracey, Judith, Vicki, Stacey, Juanita, Marta, Andrew, Terry (storyteller par excellence), Elana, Rain, Shirley, Zoe, and to all the others too numerous to mention by name. We quested on the mountain when we heard the call from Spirit, held the Fire to support the questors, and kept the traditions alive.

To Liliana, Tim, Yvonne, Nina, Michelle, Pari, Terri, Sarah, Tracey, Shawn, Jean, Paula, and Cheri – you stretched me and showed me how to be a better teacher, healer and human being.

To Jamie Sams — although we have never met in the physical — my heartfelt love and gratitude for your personal journey and beautifully written words. You spoke in a language my soul was yearning to hear and I wouldn't be where I am today without your generous offerings about the native ways to all of us in the Rainbow Tribe.

To all the women who have sat in the Clan Mother Circles in Houston, Hendersonville, Asheville, Winston Salem and Leicester, UK. We explored the teachings of the Native Sisterhood together, and I am forever grateful for all the journeys together around the Seneca Wheel of Truth.

To Nan Hall Linke for introducing me to the Feminine Journey and guiding me into the depths of the Divine Feminine, and to the other knowledgeable teachers and analysts at The Jung Center in Houston, Texas.

To Naomi and Kate of the Sacred Trust for sharing the teachings of the Way of the Melissae with such power and truth, and to all the women of the Lemniscate who touched my heart with your stories and wisdom.

To all the ones in the United Kingdom who have welcomed me and these native teachings. I have been deeply moved by the ceremonies we experienced together at Stonehenge, Chalice Well, the Tor, Avebury, Stones of Stenness, Ring of Brodgar and all the other sacred sites and stone circles.

To all the women and men who have trusted me with your beautiful hearts in the Calling Ceremony - thank you for your courage, your willingness to go deep within and for sharing your stories, small and large, so that others may benefit from your experience.

To my first spiritual tribe in the Inner Peace Movement - your camaraderie and friendship paved the way for all my future spiritual journeys.

To my imaginative and mindful writing partner, Cheryl Schirillo-Johnson for your steadfast belief in me and this material. May our fruitful writing sessions continue for a very long time!

To Cassandra Miosic for being so wise and loving and an extraordinary copy editor. Your encouraging words always brightened my day, and your spiritual depth and skillful editing enhanced my voice.

To Nina, Cheryl, Elaine, Carol, Lynn, Prema, Sue and my husband, Subash for taking the time and energy to read different drafts and bits of the manuscript. Your ideas and insights were invaluable and kept me on the right track.

To Cienna Delan Grady for your exquisite eye, tender heart and making me look my best!

To Sharon Hardin for your magical way with watercolors, translating what's in my head and heart into gorgeous artwork. Your warmth and enthusiasm are equal to your skill.

To Bhaktirasa at Inword Publishing for being a true spiritual wayshower and taking on the interior layout as well as designing the book cover so this book could be birthed in the Spring. You are a joy to work with, and I value our friendship immensely.

To my mom, Betty Jane Houtzer for being such a strong mama bear and to my dad, Robert Walter Grady for your unconditional love and for being my first example of what a feminist looks like. I know you both have been loving us and celebrating our lives from the other side because a little hummingbird told me so. To my grandmothers, Wealthy April Diedrich and Doris Lucille Burden, for your loving laps when I was little and for the inner feminine strength it took to live your life true to yourself in your time and place. To my sister Cynthia and my niece Cienna for all your love, laughter and understanding, and to my brother Jon, nephew Aaron, and niece Adrienne for your perseverance and warrior spirits.

To my son, Indigo Bear for choosing me to be your mom and sharing your gifts and abilities with generosity, impeccability and wisdom. You make my heart sing!

And to Subash, my Soul Companion, my Beloved – being with you has been the most loving and exhilarating journey that I could have ever envisioned. My Beautiful Talking Moon, I'm so grateful for the love we share and the heart connection that brought us together.

To the Medicine Ancestors and the Thirteen Original Clan Mothers for your unceasing support and encouragement, to my Spirit Guides and Animal Totems for teaching me with such profound love and acceptance, and to all beings in the Cosmos in all the myriad physical and non-physical forms of life that you inhabit. Deep gratitude that we are all on this journey together – Namaste and Wah Doh.

Robin White Star
March 14, 2017
Year of Wholehearted Kindness

About the Author

Robin White Star heard the Blue Ridge Mountains call to her in dream journeys, urging her to relocate to Western North Carolina in 1995. There she met and began her apprenticeship with Will Rockingbear, a healer and medicine man of Cherokee descent. For over 17 years, in the oral tradition, White Star absorbed the ceremonies and healing traditions of The Beauty Way that Rockingbear taught and embodied so well. These teachings augmented the spiritual journey she began at the age of thirteen while in training with the Inner Peace Movement.

Through her joyful presence, humor and keen intuitive insight, White Star offers indigenous wisdom ways to women and men who desire an intimate, authentic relationship with themselves, their Beloveds, and with all members of the Planetary Family. Highly regarded as a spiritual guide and healer, White Star often travels to the United Kingdom to teach and conduct ceremonies with her apprentices and students. To feed the holy, ceremonies are offered at sacred sites in the US and abroad, honoring the Medicine Ancestors and Spirits of the Land. White Star's shamanic drumming CD, *Medicine Ancestors*, creates an energetic "spirit canoe" for gentle and powerful inner dream journeys.

Robin White Star is the founder of Flower Eagle Medicine Lodge located near the foothills of the Blue Ridge Mountains in Winston-Salem, NC. She resides there with her husband, one furry feline, a turtle labyrinth in her backyard, and her beloved Standing Ones, the Tree People. Visit her website www.flowereagle.com for a full listing of ceremonies, healing work and ongoing circles.

Made in the USA
Monee, IL
20 January 2020